All Aboard

the old station nursery

First published in 2009 by
The Old Station Nursery Ltd
7 Park Road, Faringdon
Oxfordshire SN7 7BP
United Kingdom
www.TheOldStationNursery.co.uk

INVESTOR IN PEOPLE

Text © 2009 Sarah Steel
Photography © 2009 Mazz Image
Design © 2009 Mazz Image / www.PaloAltoMedia.com

Cataloguing in Publication Data: a catalogue record of this book is available from the British Library.

ISBN 978-0-9562535-0-7

Print Production managed by
Wrenshaws Ltd
www.Wrenshaws.co.uk

Printed in England

PEFC

PEFC/16-33-366

All Aboard

for fun & activities with

the old station nursery

words by Sarah Steel

photography by Mazz Image

FOREWORD

At the National Day Nurseries Association (NDNA) we are constantly hearing about how much children enjoy their time at nursery and all of the great fun activities that they are able to take part in. From growing plants and vegetables outdoors, to getting messy and baking play dough indoors, each part of their day is filled with the love and enthusiasm of the nursery staff and this shines through day after day, week after week. The question "What have you done at nursery today?" is rarely greeted with the same response twice in one week.

Parents often refer to nursery carers as 'extended family' and we all know the importance of making the transition between nursery and home life as smooth as possible. This is why we feel that it is great news for families that this book has been put together. Here parents and carers are given some tips and techniques on how to take nursery life into the home to share and enjoy experiences.

Sarah, a true champion of high-quality nursery care and a busy working mum, is in an excellent position to share some of her tips, advice and experiences with parents, carers and families. She has worked closely with NDNA for many years and has earned a great deal of respect within the sector, not to mention her many awards! She is an advocate of workforce development, leadership and management, and above all, she believes in making sure that all children lead fun, active, stimulating lives from birth onwards.

Today there is a greater than ever emphasis on the importance of recognising each child's individuality, natural ability and strengths. This book certainly provides a great foundation to do this through fantastic, messy, interactive and fun-filled activities, games and songs. Throughout the book, some activities make great links back to the Early Years Foundation Stage (EYFS), such as recognising and linking appropriate sounds and letters when playing 'word bingo'. This is a great element to the book as when parents, carers and families are able to recognise such developments in the home, it makes communication and consistency of care much easier to manage. This ensures that all of the child's carers, regardless of their environment, are acting in the best interests of the individual child.

NDNA is always extremely proud of the hard work and dedication shown by nurseries and nursery carers across the UK, and the high-quality care they are able to deliver to almost one million children. We know that you as parents and carers feel the same.

We are extremely pleased that Sarah has taken this step to share her expertise and sincerely hope that you find this book as much fun and a delight to read as we did!

Now get stuck in and get messy!

Purnima Tanuka
Chief Executive
National Day Nurseries Association
www.ndna.org.uk

INTRODUCTION

After a 7 year career in the Army, I left to have my second child, Jessica and spent some time at home enjoying her and her 2 year old brother, Harry. Having used a nursery for 2 years, I sometimes found it hard to provide the non-stop entertainment that was available at nursery so Harry continued doing a few sessions just to keep him busy and give me a bit of a break once Jess was born.

During this time I became increasingly interested in daycare and when we learnt our family were moving to Oxfordshire, I started looking at the local nurseries with a view to going back to work. However, I was really disappointed when couldn't find anywhere I liked in the area, resulting in one of those, "Well, I'm sure I could do that" moments which can be so dangerous! Consequently, The Old Station Nursery opened in Faringdon, Oxfordshire in 2002 to care for 60 children in a 'home from home' environment which I wanted for my children.

Since then the company has grown rapidly and we now have 13 nurseries around the UK and have been recognised with several national and local awards. The ethos is still the same: each nursery should be friendly, caring and supportive to the whole family, as I know only too well how hard it is to 'do it all'. Whether you are a single parent, have one or both parents working, and whether you have family on the doorstep or miles away, parenthood is hard work and we all need a bit of support.

My children have attended some of my nurseries, after-school and holiday clubs and are my best advisors. They have frequently asked if we can do some of the things that they have tried at nursery at home and have begged and borrowed home-made play dough and other favourite activities to take home. At the same time, I have written bi-monthly parent newsletters for several years, featuring some of our favourite ideas to make and do, so that they can carry the activities out at home. From this, the idea for *All Aboard* was born and it has been great fun rounding up recipes and activities from all the nurseries within our group. The children were more than happy to demonstrate the recipes and to be photographed, so you can rest assured that every single one has been tested thoroughly by very demanding subjects.

Sometimes days at home with little people can seem long and challenging and I hope that this book will give you a little inspiration if you are wondering what to do with them. There really is something for all occasions and I very much hope that you get as much enjoyment out of trying the ideas as we have all had putting this book together.

As parents, grandparents and carers we are sometimes bombarded with advice and new research, leaving us unsure as to what we should really be doing to give our children the best start in life. This book draws on current guidance provided for the early education of children 5 and under, and is presented in a clear and simple format, based on practical examples that everyone can follow.

So, jump aboard for our exciting journey and enjoy some mess, noise and a lot of fun!

Sarah Steel
The Old Station Nursery Ltd

ACTIVITIES & RECIPES

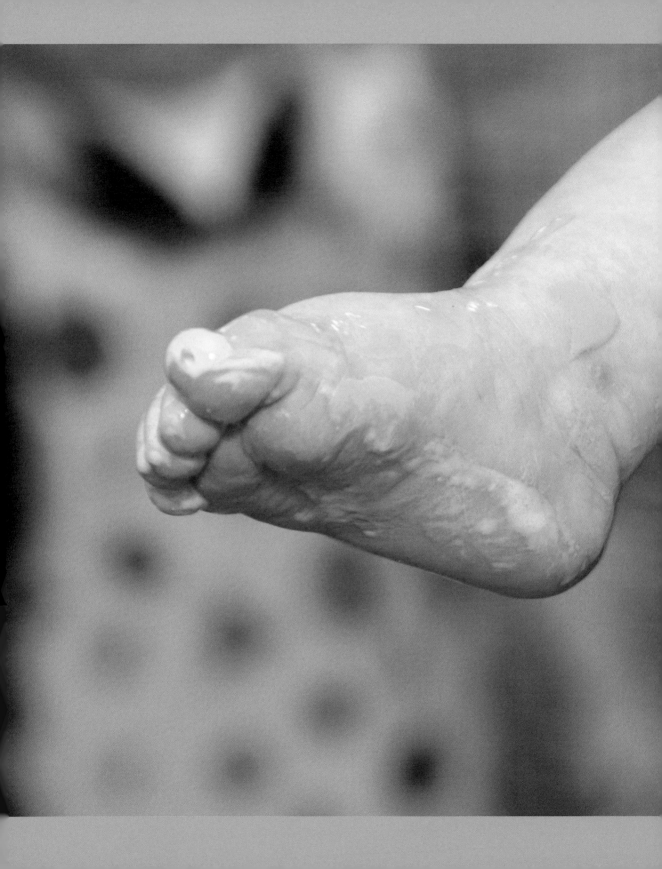

PAINTING
AND
COLOUR

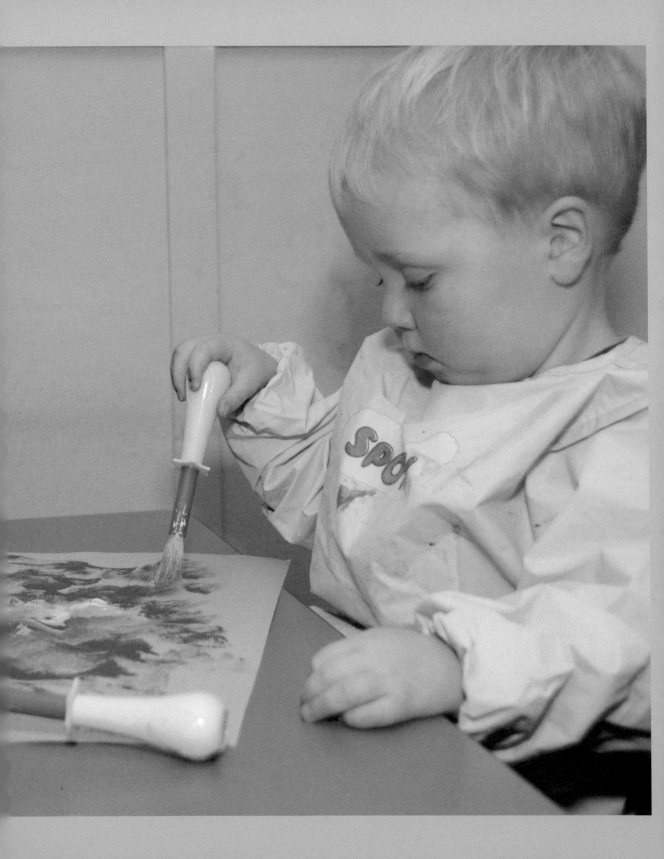

One of the most popular activities with children at our nurseries is painting. We have an easel up in most rooms with paints available for the children to use whenever they feel like it. This might not be possible – or desirable – at home, where you need to contain the mess a little more, but there are lots of activities you can do together that involve paint and colour. Most are fairly messy, but this makes them a great thing to take outside if the weather is reasonable. Don't always assume that just because it's not warm and sunny that outdoor activities aren't a good idea – we have had a lot of fun using large paintbrushes and a tub of water to 'paint' the outdoor fences or the brick work, wrapped up in coats and hats in the middle of the winter.

Do use the lovely mixing of colours to introduce some new vocabulary to your child and see how many new colours you can name. Budding scientists may be inspired by the change in texture in the paint when you add soapflakes or washing up liquid and you can both enjoy the squelch of paint between your fingers and toes.

Hand and Foot Painting

Children love to get really involved with activities and generally the messier they get, the better. My children have always enjoyed finger painting and hand printing, but whenever they spent rainy days with my mother, they loved to 'go large' and use their hands and feet to paint on a large roll of disused wallpaper, held down at each end with masking tape. On sunny days this activity transferred outside and the ultimate was to do it with a selection of friends or cousins, so everyone could compare hand and footprints and autograph their own set, Hollywood Walk of Fame style!

Equipment

Powder paint mixed up with water to a yoghurt-like
    consistency or ready-mix paint
A series of large containers, such as empty ice-cream cartons or polystyrene
    trays which fruit comes in from the supermarket
A large roll of paper – disused wallpaper is great, or you can buy
    rolls from craft and toy shops or on-line
Masking tape
Large paintbrushes, one per colour of paint
A washing up bowl full of warm, soapy water
A towel (not white!)

Method

Cut off a long strip of paper, preferably between 1 and 2 metres in length, and use masking tape to fix the corners to the floor. Place different colour paints in the trays or pots and then get your child to take off socks and shoes and sit at one end. You can either get them to dip their feet straight into the paint (not for the squeamish) or you can help them to paint their feet with the brushes, although you will probably get lots of complaints that it tickles.

If they aren't keen to go straight to feet, you can always warm up with hands and encourage them to press them firmly on to the paper. It can be fun to walk the length of the paper and see how the paint fades, or your child may have their own idea of what sort of pattern they want to create.

You can repeat this many times with combinations of hands and feet and you may even be persuaded to join in as well, just to compare the size of your feet and hands to theirs.

Tips

Always have the warm water ready before you start, with a towel, as it is usually hard to tell how long an activity will last.

Don't be tempted to be too prescriptive – it is better for them to enjoy it for 5 minutes than to get fed up with 20, even though you may feel that it has taken longer to set up and clear up than the time they actually do it for. In reality, particularly with under 3s, this is usually the case.

A 4 year old may get really engrossed and want to do it again and again, but they may take equal pleasure in producing one set of prints that they are happy with and then want to move on to something else.

It is not unreasonable to expect them to take some part in the clearing up – perhaps you could get them to rinse out the brushes and paint trays in the sink, so they feel they are 'washing up' just like you.

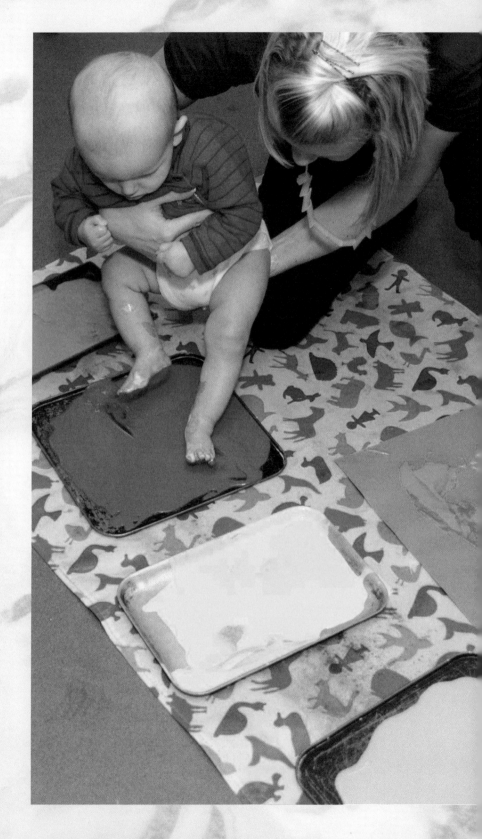

Puddle Painting

This is a really fun way of using colours with water and seeing how they mix together. It is also a great way of getting outside after some rain and splashing around with a purpose - just in case you need one!

Ingredients

Powder paint

Equipment

Medium sized paint brushes

Method

Keep the powder paint as a dry powder and sprinkle it in the middle of a puddle. Then use the paint brush to swirl it around and mix it until you have a lovely bold colour.

You can then either mix different colours in to experiment with blending colours and creating new ones, or move on to a different puddle for a different colour.

Tips

We have found that the children love this activity, it is something about being outside in their wellies and still being able to paint and be creative. Some children will spend ages just in one puddle, mixing lurid colours, whereas others like to experiment spreading the paint out and even brushing it on to walls and other surfaces.

As it is so dilute it can easily be rinsed off, or you can just wait for the next shower. If you have any large decorating brushes, these are great for painting a larger area with the coloured water and can also provide a lot of entertainment.

Marble Painting

I'm sure many of us have memories of different sorts of painting activities that we carried out at home or playgroup. At nursery, we always have paints out in the pre-school room and children are encouraged to wait until there is a space at an easel, put an apron on and paint whatever they want to.

The emphasis over recent years has moved away from us suggesting what they might want to paint – 'let's all paint a flower' – to children just expressing themselves freely and experimenting with textures and colours. This frequently results in less appealing creations from an adult perspective and it is surprising how often an all black picture emerges! This activity is rather easier to do at home, particularly if you don't have an easel or room for large pieces of paper. Here a marble is used in a tray to create interesting patterns and then a print is taken.

Ingredients

Powder paint mixed up with water to a yoghurt-like consistency
or ready-mix paint

Equipment

A tray (preferably plastic and with raised edges)
A4 paper
1 or 2 marbles (glass or plastic)

Method

Place a splodge of paint in the middle of the tray and spread it out with a paint brush in a random manner. If it is too thick to spread easily, add a little water and brush it to the edges: the whole tray does not have to be covered, you can experiment to get the best results. Place a marble in the tray and roll it around in the paint. Your child may enjoy doing this with their hands, which is just fine, but do remember if they are still at the stage where everything goes in their mouth, you may wish to roll the marble around then put it out of reach before starting the next stage. However, for children aged 3 upwards, or if you are closely supervising, they will have great fun rolling the marble around and watching the patterns it makes in the paint.

Next remove the marble and lay a piece of A4 paper face down in the tray, gently pressing down. Encourage your child to peel back the edge and see what pattern the marble has made in the paint, which is now printed on the paper. Place the painting to dry, add more paint and more marbles as required and experiment with the results.

Tips

Whenever you are doing a painting activity, you will end up with bits of soggy paper littered around your kitchen. It may be worth buying a cheap clothes airer, if you have room, and keep it with a few clothes pegs to use for drying paintings on.

We also use lines of string, like washing lines, inside or out, to display and dry paintings on. It is a great way of reinforcing your child's self-worth by displaying their 'work' and they take real pleasure in seeing that you value what they have made.

Table Top Painting

This painting activity is always a hit, perhaps because the children feel there is something slightly illegal about making such a mess on the table! It can be done with the very youngest children – we will sit babies in a high chair and use the tray in front of them for painting on, keeping a close eye to try and avoid paint being eaten. With slightly older children we would sit them at a table, making sure they are wearing an apron.

Ingredients

Powder paint mixed up with water to a yoghurt-like consistency or ready-mix paint

Equipment

A wipeable work-surface, or plastic sheet over a wooden surface
A4 paper

Method

This couldn't be more simple to do at home and you can involve more than one child of any age. Just make sure that plenty of water is ready for hand-washing afterwards. Squeeze a spoonful size of paint on to the table and then encourage your child to put their fingers into the paint and spread it out in front of them. They can then use their fingers to make wiggles, lines and patterns and whenever they are happy, you use the A4 paper to take a print of their creation.

You can mix colours, make waves and straight lines and generally be as creative as you like. When you have finished, just use an old dishcloth to clean the paint off the table or plastic sheet.

Tips

The finished results can either be kept whole and put up on display, or you can use them to make collages, cut into shapes or as part of a topic that you might want to discuss. We often make pictures of beach or holiday scenes during the summer and you could use blue paint to make sea colour and yellow paint for sand, then draw fish shapes on the top once it is all dry, to give a sea scene.

Soapflake Finger Painting

It is handy to have a thicker consistency of paint for really good finger painting, as children can find normal ready-mix or powder paint rather frustrating as it can slide off fingers and not be thick enough. This very simple recipe will give you a nice, thick texture of paint, which will keep for weeks in an airtight container and will also give a limited amount of mess as it is not so runny. Ideal if you have visiting children to entertain on a wet day.

Ingredients

1 cup soap flakes (from supermarket or chemists)
1 cup cornflour
1 litre boiling water
Powder paint or ready mix paint, sufficient to add colour

Equipment

Large mixing bowl
A wipeable work-surface, or plastic sheet over a wooden surface
A4 or larger paper

Method

Dissolve the cornflour in a small amount of the water and then add the remaining boiling water. Boil until the mixture is thick. Take it off the heat and beat in the soapflakes. Add a small spoonful of paint or powder to give the desired colour and mix well. Once cool, store the mixture in an airtight container and it should keep for several weeks.

Tips

Even the youngest of children enjoy finger painting and it can be a great way to extend learning from other activities you may be involved in. Many of the favourite nursery rhymes involve using your fingers for actions, such as 'Incy Wincy Spider' and you may want to then make up some black paint and make leggy spiders with your fingers. Some bright yellow paint would make a great sun and you could continue to sing and do the actions as you paint. Counting is also a natural activity with fingers and toes, so you could also use different colours and try counting how many prints you can make with each hand.

Spaghetti Painting

Painting with fruit and vegetables is a well-known way of using foodstuffs to add interest to craft activities and the variety within your kitchen is huge. This recipe uses dried spaghetti – a value brand from any supermarket will do fine – and children will enjoy the texture of the spaghetti as much as the painting itself.

Ingredients

Powder paint mixed up with water to a yoghurt-like consistency or ready-mix paint

Equipment

A large tray or waterproof work-surface
50g of cooked, drained and cooled spaghetti
A4 paper

Method

Mix the cooled, cooked spaghetti with the paint, preferably with lots of help from your child. Don't be tempted to see this as just a pre-cursor to the painting, it is an intrinsic, if very messy, part of the activity. Once the spaghetti is evenly coated in paint, take strands out one at a time and use them to make shapes on the paper. You may wish to lay them directly on the paper and pull them along to get different results, or you may wish to put them on to a tray and then take a print with the paper.

Tips

This is a really simple activity but can be used to help develop particular areas of learning that you are interested in. With younger children (under 2s) this would just be a messy, sensual activity; with 2-3 year olds we might encourage them to make different shapes (circles, triangles, squares) with the spaghetti and then print them off on paper and cut them out when they are dry. Pre-schoolers might like to see if they can make number or letter shapes with the spaghetti and could be helped to make a number line or alphabet frieze to put on the wall

Splatter Painting

This activity is not one for the faint-hearted, but can be great fun with more than one child and is absolutely ideal for a fabulous Bonfire Night picture. Unless you have plenty of room inside, I would strongly recommend you do it outside, as children do have a tendency to get carried away with the splattering part.

Ingredients

Powder paint or ready-mix paint, in a variety of colours, with a fairly runny consistency
Large sheets of paper

Equipment

Medium sized paint brushes

Method

Fasten the paper to a wall, preferably outside. You may find masking tape the easiest way to do this, so you can use a fence or wall. Make sure the children are wearing old clothes or an apron and then give them a pot of paint with a brush in it and encourage them to flick the loaded paint-brush at the paper, experimenting to see how the paint splatters depending on how they move the brush. You can use several different colours, one after another to build up a multi-coloured picture. Once it is dry you may like to make a bonfire in one corner using twigs and leaves and you will have a really authentic Bonfire Night picture.

Tips

It can be really time consuming at home to set up a messy activity like this one and sometimes you may feel that you spend much longer setting it up and clearing up afterwards than your child actually spends doing it. However, try to involve them in the setting up, by getting them to measure out paint, whilst you talk about the different colours. Even getting the paper up on the wall is a learning experience as you can discuss why different types of tape might work better on the rough or smooth surface of the wall. Again, when you finish, washing up the paint pots can be as fun as the actual painting and if you don't want your kitchen sink multi-coloured, just fill a washing up bowl or bucket with warm water and bring it outside so your child can do the first rinse. Mine always spent far longer washing up the pots as it involved making potions and brews and gave me time to clear up other parts of the activity.

SOUNDS, WORDS AND NUMBERS

At nursery we refer to this area of learning as communication, language and literacy and it is a really important part of a child's development. There is so much that adults can do to support speech, listening skills and eventually reading and writing and it can be incorporated into every part of the day. This chapter aims to highlight some games and activities that parents can carry out with their children to promote these skills.

Being able to communicate is vital to children as they are sociable beings who need to build relationships and develop friendships. In order to become skilful communicators they need to have warm and loving relationships with their carers and these are built on trust. Lots of these games rely on close physical contact, listening and talking and enjoying sounds together.

Parents automatically have the greatest knowledge of their child's words and expressions through time spent together, but many of these activities can also help friends, relatives and grandparents to enjoy time with children and will help them to develop a wider circle of trusted people.

Finger Puppets

Puppets can be a great way of nurturing the creative side to your child, as they can be used for songs and rhymes, for making up short plays and for interacting with other children. You can buy finger and hand puppets very easily now and if you build up a collection of them, you will always be ready for a singing session. Even the shyest child will often respond to a puppet – we have French lessons at nursery and 3 year olds will quickly learn that they have to say 'Toc, toc, toc, qui est la?' to meet whichever puppet is hiding in the teacher's bag. Here is a suggestion for making 2 very simple bird finger puppets, which you can then use for 'Two little dicky birds'.

Equipment

Different coloured felt squares
PVA glue
Needle and thread
Buttons or sequins
Scissors

Method

Take the felt and draw on it a chick shape, with a large round for the body and smaller round on top for the head. The whole thing should be about twice the size of your finger. Cut two identical shapes and then either glue the edges together, or if you have the time, sew around to fasten the edges, leaving the bottom edge open for your finger.

Decorate the front of the puppet with a small triangle of contrasting coloured felt, glued on as a beak. Add buttons, beads or sequins for eyes, and you will have your first bird. Repeat with different coloured felt to make a second bird, so that you will be able to identify Peter and Paul during the rhyme.

Show your child the 2 finger puppets and tell them the rhyme:

> "Two little dickie birds, sitting on a wall,
> One called Peter, one called Paul.
> Fly away Peter, fly away Paul,
> Come back Peter, come back Paul."

Then swap the puppets over and let them have a go!

Tips

With small babies, you can just use puppets to dance to the rhythm of a piece of music and to catch their attention. You can imitate familiar sounds during rhymes, such as animal noises and they will soon begin to join in with the sounds and actions. Try action songs like 'Head, shoulders, knees and toes' and introduce them to words which describe sounds, such as soft, quiet, loud, fast and slow.

Try to expose your child to a wide variety of music from different cultures and genres and tell them more about what they are hearing and how the sound is made.

Shakers and Rhythm

Children learn best when they are doing something that engages as many senses as possible, so singing or dancing and using percussion instruments can be a great way to enhance language development. Even young babies enjoy gentle rhythms such as being rocked and sung to and they also enjoy following the familiar routine of a rhyme with actions, such as *Round and round the garden*. These different types of shakers are very easy to make, but will last indefinitely and can be used with nursery rhymes, singing and dancing.

Equipment

Empty cardboard containers
Small plastic drinks bottles
Uncooked rice or lentils
Greaseproof paper or plain paper
Ready mix paint

Kitchen roll tubes
Yoghurt pots
Elastic bands
Paintbrushes
Scissors
Sticky tape

Method

Simply choose your container (such as a kitchen roll) and seal one end with sticky tape. If you are using a cardboard tube, then cover the base with paper and secure well with sellotape. Pour in a tablespoon of lentils or rice, keeping it away from small children who might be tempted to put it in their mouths. Then seal the top, either with more paper or the lid, if it has one one. You will now have a shaker, ready to decorate as you wish.

You can either paint the container or collage it with pictures from a magazine, covered in tape strips to secure them. You can be as adventurous as you like, or just get on and use the shakers as they are. Try making several different types of shaker, using a variety of containers and experiment to show your child how you get a different noise from each container, as well as with different fillings.

Tips

By linking words with physical movements, you will help your child's language to develop, so try using your shakers for actions songs, such as Wheels on the bus. They can experiment with combining the rhythm from the shaker with the words they are singing and you can try speeding up and slowing down. You could also try The Grand Old Duke of York, varying the shaker rhythm to match the speed of marching. Be prepared to repeat favourite songs several times and remember that songs and rhymes with repeated choruses and refrains allow children to anticipate what is coming and join in.

Word Bingo

One of the most discussed areas of the Early Years Foundation Stage has been the subject of linking sounds and letters and what are reasonable expectations for children at each stage. There has been much debate about the use of phonics in helping children to learn to read, but whatever the experts may say, most parents will recognise the importance of speaking to their children and using words and sounds to help children to develop and express themselves. There are numerous games that you can buy in shops like the Early Learning Centre which can help you to focus on word play, but you can also make some very simple games up at home. This game of Word Bingo can be enjoyed by 3 year olds upwards and you can theme it around current interests.

Equipment

8 pieces of A4 card
Ruler
PVA glue or glue stick
Old magazines
Felt pens

Method

Take 4 pieces of card and divide into 6 squares, using the ruler to draw a grid. Then, sort through the magazines and cut out 6 nice, clear pictures of objects which your child recognises and is interested in. For example; a pair of shoes, a dog, a spoon, a cake etc. This can all be done with your child and try and involve them in the choice of items so that you know they will recognise them. Stick the objects on to one piece of card in each square, so that you end up with a grid filled in with 6 different objects. You now need to repeat this for each of the 4 cards, so that you have 4 completed bingo cards, each with 6 different objects on. Underneath the object write the name of the object in clear handwriting, all in lower case. Now take the remaining 4 pieces of card, draw an identical grid on to each, as you did before, but now cut along the lines to give you 6 pieces from each card. On these you now write the word for the object on each of the completed bingo cards. As with the bingo cards, use lower case letters, written very clearly by hand, to make it as easy as possible for your child to recognise the letters.

Now you are ready to go. You can play with up to 4 people, but if you play with fewer, make sure you use the corresponding bingo cards and smaller cards. Place the smaller cards face down on the table and have a bingo card each, face up. Take turns to turn over one of the smaller cards so that you can all see it and see if it matches any of the objects on your bingo card. If it does, you take the card and place it on top of the picture on your bingo card. If it doesn't match, turn it back over and the next player has a go. The winner is the first person to cover all the objects on their bingo card with the smaller cards.

Tips

This game is really a combination of bingo and a memory game and can work really well with children as young as 3, but can also be made more complicated for older children. Use the game to encourage your child to recognise the sounds of the letters that they hear at the beginning of the words and highlight if any of them are letters within their own name. Get them to match the first letter of the words with those words on their bingo card and then read them the word so they can then link the word with the picture.

Alliteration is a great way of helping them to grasp letter sounds, so if you have a picture of a shoe, then say 'sh-sh-sh-shoe and see if they can suggest any other objects that start with 'sh'. Rhymes also engage even the youngest children, so if you have a picture of a pig, then experiment with all the words that rhyme with 'pig'. The words can be real or imaginary, it all helps your child to link the sounds and letters together.

At nursery each room might have a 'rhyme of the week', which is written out and laminated and then used every day. Whist the adults may get a little tired of it by Friday, it is a great way of building familiarity and confidence and even babies will recognise the rhyme after several times and will anticipate some of the sounds and actions. You can do this at home too, changing when your child is bored or discovers a new one they like better.

Story Sacks

Most children have a favourite book which they like to hear again and again and often you find that the characters from this story overflow into other areas of daily life. My husband amazed one lady as he helped her carry her pushchair up the stairs in the underground, when he recited the whole of *The Owl Babies* which her toddler son was clutching. "Are you the author?" she asked in surprise, "No," he replied, "I've just read it every evening for at least a year!'. If your child has a favourite book, or if you would like to expand their repertoire, then you could make up a story sack to engage them in the story and characters.

Equipment

Drawstring bag (plimsoll bags from a shoe shop are ideal)
or a fabric bag if you like sewing
A popular child's book
Props that will support the book

Method

A story sack is simply a collection of items which extend the range of a book to allow you to have a really nice discussion around the story and play some games which develop the themes in the book. You can pick different books depending on their current interests and if you have something major going on in your life, like maybe moving house, or having another baby, then a book on this subject could be the centre of the story sack. Put all the items together in the bag and then when your child asks for the story, you can get the sack out and explore the contents together. It can be a different experience each time, depending on what part they decide they would like to focus on.

Tips

The book which you choose for a story sack will determine exactly what activities might fit well; The Very Hungry Caterpillar can be used on many fronts to help your child to explore new concepts; the lifecycle of the caterpillar is fascinating to children and you could even consider hatching your own butterflies (there are some great 'butterfly houses' available to buy now).

The food that the caterpillar eats is also a good way of introducing the 'five a day' recommendations for fruit and vegetable and also general nutritional concepts. Counting is an integral part of the story and the repetition will really help young children with this. Whatever you choose, add items to the story sack as you think of them, so there is occasionally something new in there to amuse and interest them.

Some examples of Story Sacks include:

The Gruffalo
by Julia Donaldson
and Alex Scheffler

A jigsaw puzzle of the characters
A mouse and fox mask so you
can role play from the book
A piece of fabric which feels
like the skin of a snake
A piece of bark
An owl soft-toy

The Bear Hunt
by Michael Rosen

A cuddly bear
A snow storm
(shakeable globe)
A home made shaker
(to make swishy-swashy sound)
A pair of old wellies
(for tramping through the mud)
A pair of binoculars
(made from 2 toilet rolls)

The Very Hungry Caterpillar
by Eric Carle

Some plastic or wooden fruit
A picture of a butterfly
or a finger puppet butterfly
7 cards with the days of the
week written on them
Some colouring cards with
pictures of the food that is
mentioned in the book and
some crayons

Number and Word Rhymes

Poetry and play have been linked throughout history and many of us will have rhymes that we remember from our childhood and children may also enjoy asking grandparents and great-grandparents what they remember from their childhood. Most of the games will involve a rhyme as this is what helps us to remember it for so long. This power can be harnessed to engage the youngest children and they will join in rhymes with glee. As your child gets older, use rhyme to help develop numeracy and literacy skills in a fun way. Even our 21st century, high-tech children love a good game of hide and seek!

Suggested games and rhymes

Hide and seek: start with counting to 10 with younger children and once they are happy with this you can increase it up to at least 20. Remind them of the connection between how many you count to and how long they get to hide. This game can be played inside and out, whatever the weather and can be done with just 2 of you or lots of friends. The counter closes their eyes and counts to 10, calling "*Coming, ready or not!*" when then get to 10. In the meantime everyone else hides and then has to be found by the counter. You can vary this by playing by torchlight on a late winter afternoon (maybe hiding in pairs for those not so keen on the dark) or if you only have a small space outside or in, try blindfolding the counter and encourage them to use their listening skills to find the hiders.

If you want to add another twist, try teaching your child the numbers from 1 to 10 in a different language, saying them out loud like this is a great way of learning them and more fun than just reciting them. We teach French at nursery and even the just 3 year olds quickly pick up the numbers. If you have been on holiday somewhere or have friends or relations who speak a different language, they might like to teach your child the numbers specially for this game.

Ring a ring o' roses: this old classic allegedly stems back to the Black Death when everyone would carry a posy of herbs to fend off the contagious disease. Despite its sinister connections, it is great with children and easily remembered. Form a circle, from 2 people upwards, holding hands and chant: *'Ring a ring o' roses, a pocketful of posies, atishoo, atishoo, we all fall down'*. At this point you all sit on the floor. Subsequent verses vary enormously from area to area, but we tend to use *'The cows are in the meadow, eating buttercups, atishoo, atishoo, they all jump up.'* Or, *'Fishes in the water, fishes in the sea, we all jump up, with a one, two, three!'*

1 potato, 2 potato: this is a great game for waiting around somewhere when space is limited. You can play with just 2 people and the first makes a fist and holds it out, thumb end facing upwards, saying *"1 potato"*. The other person then puts their fist on top, saying *"2 potato"*. You carry this on until you get to 6 and then the next fist is *"7 potato more"*. The next person is then *"1 big, bad spud"* and is the loser. If you play regularly with your child, they will soon realise that whoever starts will always be the loser, but as soon as you add a third person in, it makes the outcome less obvious and they never seem to tire of it. The same goes for the many playground choosing games *Ippy dippy dation, my operation* and others that you may remember, to choose who will be the leader for a particular game. By introducing them to the concept of *1 potato, 2 potato*, it helps them to grasp the idea.

Suggested games and rhymes, continued...

Here we go round the mulberry bush: this game is lovely with babies upwards, as they can anticipate the different verses and will learn to join in the actions of everyday activities.
If you are a bit rusty, here are some of the verses:

Here we go round the mulberry bush, the mulberry bush, the mulberry bush,
Here we go round the mulberry bush, on a cold and frosty morning.

This is the way we wash our face, wash our face, wash our face,
This is the way we wash our face, on a cold and frosty morning.

This is the way we brush our hair, brush our hair, brush our hair,
This is the way we brush our hair, on a cold and frosty morning.

This is the way we jump up and down, jump up and down, jump up and down,
This is the way we jump up and down, on a cold and frosty morning.

You can obviously add your own verses involving any routine activities that you like. Mime the actions as you sing and encourage your child to join in too. You might feel a bit silly at first, but it doesn't last for long! With pre-school children you could then go on to look at which letter sounds start some of the words, such as the 'b' for brush, or 'j' for jumping up and down and you could show them how to write them on a piece of paper or paint them on a picture.

Tips

When you are singing or chanting rhymes with children, think about how the language is passed on, not just through the words but with the way in which the game is actually structured. There are lots of ways in which mathematical concepts can be introduced in this way, using phrases such as: "make a circle", "move closer together", "stretch your arms a bit further out to make the circle bigger", or "squeeze up close together".

If you have an odd number of people playing, ask the children to get into pairs and then discuss why one person doesn't have a partner. If you ask them to get in to 3s, does the problem disappear? Problem solving starts at a very early age......

A favourite poem will never fade in the sun, it won't blow away in the wind and it certainly won't get wet; it is the ultimate outdoor resource for literacy!

Poetry and outdoor play have been linked for centuries. The oral tradition began outdoors, and for many adults the poetry of the street was an integral part of childhood. Once gently prompted, adults tend to remember a wide collection of poetry which usually includes a range of counting-out rhymes, skipping games, songs to be sung in a circle, playground games and rhymes associated with playing ball.

There is a tendency to think that today's children are unaware of such things, or have moved on to more sophisticated forms of play. I don't think that such a view is true, and even if it were, then teaching children such songs, rhymes and poems becomes even more important. Children need to know that playground rhymes and games are valued and that you want to hear them chanted and see them played!

Word and Number Labels

Many catalogues and shops sell sets of 'high frequency words' that you can use around the home to introduce your pre-schooler to some of the words that they will certainly encounter at school. However, it is very easy to do this yourself, by labelling key areas in the house and garden. This page gives some suggestions of what you might like to do to help your child to develop word and number skills.

Equipment

Plain card
Felt tip pens
Laminator if required
Tape

Method

Use lower case handwriting for making your labels and then use tape to fasten them around the house where your child will see them. You may like to label lots of familiar objects such as door, window, chair, pen, book etc, but also try to think of how labels can help children to think about how words and numbers are used in an every day way. For example, you could put a label next to their toothbrush with the number 1 showing, then the number of 2 next to where you keep their shoes, and maybe 3 next to their 3 favourite cuddly toys.

If you have a set of numbers from 1 to 20 in a handy place, you can use them to reinforce counting during the day. For example try:

- Saying and using number names when you are preparing vegetables or opening packets or tins in the kitchen.

- Draw their attention to numbers on coins, notes, receipts, price labels and signs when you are out shopping.

- Help them to develop simple mathematical concepts by counting how many large apples will fit into a bag, then try using smaller apples to see how many fit in now.

- Introduce vocabulary which you use for adding and subtracting, such as, "If we add 2 more biscuits to the plate, how many will we have then?" Or, "If we have 5 cakes and we take away 1, how many will we have left?"

- Use language such as 'less than' and 'more than' to develop the concept of comparison.

Tips

As adults we read all the time, looking at road signs, timetables, street signs, instructions at work, recipes and so much more. We have words all around us and it is important that we make this the case for children in both nurseries and at home, so they become comfortable and familiar with them.

At nursery we label all the pictures that children draw or paint, so they learn the letters of their name, but also encourage 'emergent writing', which may look like scribbles to you and me! However, if you put pen and paper next to the play kitchen, or chalk and a board out in the garden next to their push-along car, you may be surprised at how much it is used in role play. This all helps children to make sense of the world around them, after all, your average 3 year old could certainly tell you what to expect when you see certain fast food signs.

CRAFT
AND
MESSY PLAY

One of the main advantages of your child attending nursery must be that the majority of really messy craft activities can take place at nursery rather than at home! However, we do get lots of parents asking what we have been doing with their children – not just to get them so messy to send home, but also to have so much fun. When we opened the first nursery in Faringdon, I was amazed to see babies playing happily up to their elbows in 'gloop' – a sticky cornflour mix which is included in this chapter. Having never worked in a nursery before, I had not come across this lovely substance, which somehow seems to draw adults to it as much as children. We often put it out as an interactive display at parents' evenings and it is never left alone.

Many of these activities can be fun with either one child or several, although you do just need to be a bit more organised with more than one, particularly when it comes to the clearing up stage. I always think it's a good idea to have the next thing lined up before you start a really messy game, as once your child has tired of it, they will be looking for something else to do while you deal with the chaos they have caused. You might like to have a small snack and a drink ready, so they can sit next to you while you clear up, giving you a fighting chance of recovery. Mind you, who am I kidding, at the end of a day at home with small children you can chart the day's activities by the stream of mess throughout the house – don't worry, it's not just you!

Paper Dolls

This is an old favourite, but always gives so much pleasure. It is also another way of encouraging good scissor skills and helps to develop fine motor skills.

Equipment

Scissors
Paper – preferably A3 or other large sheets
Colouring crayons or felt-tip pens

Method

Fold the paper in a concertina, about 8-10cm wide. You can demonstrate on one piece while your child tries with another, but be prepared to help smoothing down the folds to give nice sharp lines. You can then mark out a boy or girl shape on the folded paper, making sure that the arms of the figure reach all the way to the folded edges. If it is a girl, you should make sure that the skirt also reaches the edges and for boys the feet will need to touch the edges too.

Cut around the outline and discard the spare bits of paper. Open out the concertina and you should have a lovely row of boys or girls. The fun really starts now as the children can allow their imagination to run riot, colouring, painting, glittering and decorating as they see fit.

Tips

This is a great activity to tie into a project or topic, or for a particular time of the year. If we were doing a project on 'countries of the world', it would be fun to ask the children to choose a number of countries and paint the dolls in colours of the national flags.

Older children might like to draw the national costumes. It would also be a good activity to talk about favourite sports or hobbies, colouring the dolls in favourite football strips.

Catalogue Collage

We all get inundated with catalogues and magazines these days, but rather than recycling them all, they can be a great source of fun to children. Pick a theme or topic that interests your child, then assemble a pile of magazines and spend a rainy afternoon sorting through and cutting out suitable pictures. You can do the more fiddly ones, but whatever age your child is, do encourage them to use an appropriate pair of scissors and have a go themselves.

Equipment

PVA glue
Brushes or spreaders
A4 paper or larger
Selection of magazines or catalogues

Method

Simply cut out a selection of pictures and words and use them to create a picture on the paper. Don't be too prescriptive – you may want to make a recognisable display, but younger children may just enjoy sticking random images on to a sheet. You could choose a colour theme to follow and cut out all green pictures, which will create a different effect when viewed from a distance.

Older children may enjoy filling in a word or shape with relevant pictures – try marking out the letters of 'garden' and giving each child one to fill in with photographs of plants and flowers, then arrange them on a backing sheet to make a bright display that they are really proud of.

Tips

Laminating machines are now available relatively inexpensively and can transform things that the children have made. You might like to try laminating a favourite collage to turn into a place mat for the table and these make great presents for friends and relatives. If you take lots of digital photos you may also use spare ones for children to turn into mats, as the laminating makes them much more durable.

We also laminate family photos at nursery and then attach Velcro to the back of them; the babies in particular love pulling them off and sticking them back on to a wall surface that has the Velcro on.

Spaghetti Play

Continuing my voyage of discovery about the delights of pasta for play, I was fascinated the first time I watched a group of toddlers crowded round a large tray which was full of cooked spaghetti. The spaghetti had a lovely sticky texture and a great selection of small plastic dinosaurs hidden within it. They were having a lovely time creating dens and mountains and moving the dinosaurs around this new landscape. It may seem like an unusual play medium, but if you buy 'value' brand spaghetti from the supermarket, you will get a great deal of pleasure out of a few pence worth of pasta.

Equipment

200g dried spaghetti
Boiling water for cooking the pasta
Food colouring or paint if required

Method

Cook the spaghetti as per the instructions on the packet, adding food colouring or paint to the water if you require a coloured end product. Drain well and run under cold water once it is cooked. Tip out onto a large tray and add any toys that you think will be well received and are easily washable. You may like to provide 2 different coloured piles of spaghetti (jungle and sea?) and talk to your child about what they are doing and how it feels.

Tips

This is also suitable for very young children and once babies are sitting up comfortably in a high chair, they may enjoy this too. For such young children I would leave out any colouring as they will inevitably end up eating some, but they will enjoy touching, squeezing and stretching the pasta.

For older children, it can become part of a longer running game and they may well improvise, adding favourite toys that they think might go well. Just be on hand to make encouraging noises, suggest what they might add and talk to them about the texture, smell, feel and colour.

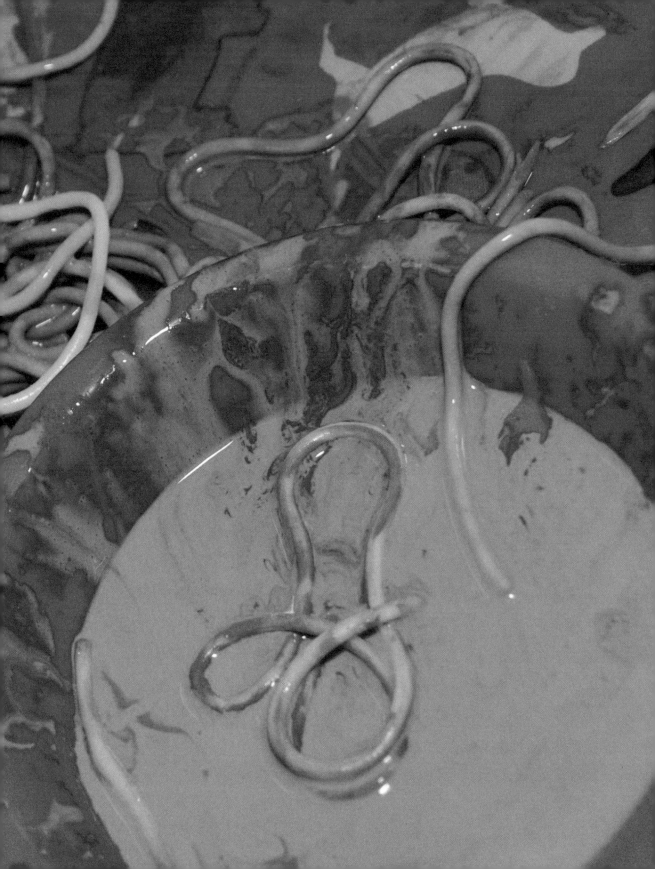

Pasta Jewellery

Before starting the nurseries, I had always rashly assumed that pasta was for eating! However, I have rapidly discovered that it is actually an essential play ingredient and is as versatile in the play room as it is in the kitchen. Here we use dried pasta for making necklaces and bracelets.

Equipment

Ready mix paint or powder paint
Dried pasta – tube shaped, such as penne
String
Scissors
Plastic threading needle

Method

If you would like a colourful piece of jewellery, first cook the pasta in some boiling water with a good squirt of paint in the water, or a large spoonful of powder paint. Cook it for about half the recommended time, usually for about 4 minutes, then drain well and rinse with cold water to cool it quickly. Drain well in a colander and then lay it out on a sheet of greaseproof paper or foil while it dries out, preferably overnight.

If you don't want to do this rather messy stage, or are short of time, just use the dried pasta without colouring it. Then, thread a large plastic needle, or if you don't have one, use a plastic drinking straw and just tie a very large knot in the end to keep the string secured. Encourage your child to thread the pasta shapes onto the string, alternating colours or using different shapes to achieve patterns.

Measure the necklace to make sure it is long enough to loop easily around the neck. Then tie it off and fasten securely. You are now ready to accessorise...!

Tips

This may seem like a fiddly way of colouring the pasta, but you can always do a few small batches at a time and as long as you make sure it dries out thoroughly after cooking, you can keep it for several weeks in an airtight container.

You can also paint it with PVA glue and sprinkle glitter on it for those with more sparkly tastes. Older children can get quite absorbed in designing the pasta 'beads' and may enjoy choosing different pasta shapes in the supermarket to use.

Putty

In most toy or joke shops you can buy small tubs of play putty, which is a deliciously gloopy mixture, with a texture somewhere between jelly and playdough. Unfortunately the shop-bought variety is not only expensive, but has a nasty tendency to spread itself around your carpets and you then have none left to play with. This recipe was created by the team at our WASPS after-school club and is a real hit with children aged from 4 up to 11. In truth, any visiting adults and also the staff team all find putty strangely addictive...a kind of stress relief....!

Ingredients

2 tablespoons of Glycerine
1 tablespoon of Borax Powder
(available at Boots or
Greenshop, see page 184)
1 pint of boiling water
2 yoghurt pots of PVA glue
Food colouring

Method

Mix together all the water and PVA glue in a bowl, preferably a plastic one. Add the food colouring to the glue/water mixture. In a separate container mix together the Borax powder and glycerine, then add this mixture to the glue/water mixture and stir continuously. The mixture will become thick and lumpy at first and will then smooth out. Leave to cool and set over night and store in an air tight container until you are ready to play with it.

This putty will keep for weeks if kept in an airtight container. If any of the mixture or the finished putty gets on clothes, you will need to keep the area damp until it can be washed. Do not allow to dry, as it turns hard and becomes difficult to get out.

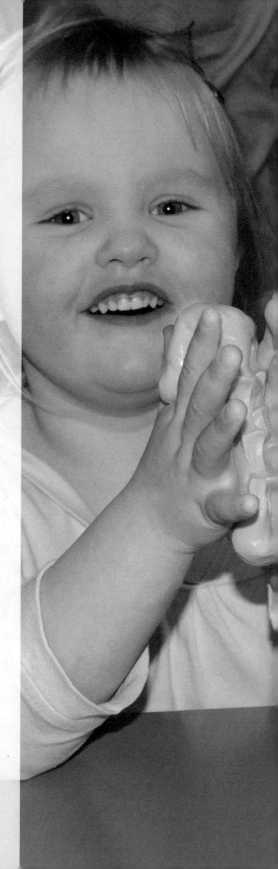

Tips

We encourage school-aged children to weigh out the ingredients for this sort of activity and it can be a mathematical or scientific exercise of any degree you wish. You might like to look up some more information about the Borax powder or glycerine on the Internet or discuss how the various ingredients react together to make a completely different texture.

For a simpler activity, encourage younger children to mix the different food colours to make the desired shade or colour. This could lead on to drawing rainbows for 2-4 year olds, or at the other end of the scale your 10 year old might like to find out more about prisms and how light is refracted into the colours of the rainbow.

Small tubs of putty make excellent going-home or goody bag presents for birthday parties if you would like to do something original – at a fraction of the cost of shop-bought varieties. You can even buy a large tube of plastic bugs and insects and spread them between the pots of gloop for super-nasty insect gloop.

Glitter Play Dough

Play dough is a real favourite with children from all ages up to adults. The texture, smell and feel of the soft substance lends itself to all sorts of creative play. My children have progressed from rolling out pretend biscuits, to making Dr Who figures and ballerinas out of it. At nursery we tend to introduce it when the children are approaching 2 years old, as much before this it is too hard trying to stop them from eating it! Most recipes for home made play dough include a fair proportion of salt; this not only deters eating but also acts as a preservative and this should keep for up to a week in the fridge as long as it is well wrapped in cling film to avoid exposure to the air.

Recipe

2 cups plain flour
1 cup salt
1 cup water
2 tbsps vegetable oil
Food colouring and glitter (as desired)

Method

Mix the flour and salt together in a mixing bowl and sprinkle in the glitter (about half a small tube will make a really sparkly batch). Make a well in the middle and add the water and oil gradually, stirring well as you pour. Once the ingredients are well mixed, add a little more water if the mixture is too stiff and then tip it on to a work surface and knead for a couple of minutes. Now you are ready to play!

Tips

Messy play is just that – messy. Try and prepare the area you are going to use so that you can be relaxed about any ingredients that will get spilt; they certainly will. If you do not have a wipeable floor surface, consider investing in a large plastic sheet or lay down some newspaper as it is not relaxing for you if you are just thinking about how much clearing up you will have to do. Collect a range of cutters, rolling pins and blunt knives that your child can use with the play dough. I have an old jar of cake candles and cake holders that have been a real hit; numerous birthday cakes have been made and 'happy birthdays' sung to teddy bears and dolls. Use the play time to talk with your child about what they are doing. How does it feel? Which colour do they like best? Can they count the number of biscuits they have cut out? Pre-school children learn best through play, not through formal teaching, so make it fun and then help them to develop concepts of numeracy and new vocabulary while they are enjoying themselves.

Gloop!

I always remember mixing up custard powder for my mother when I was a child, marvelling at the strange texture that the cornflour made when mixed with milk, that sort of 'dry, but wet' feeling. This mixture has many different names around the nurseries, but my favourite is 'gloop', as it seems to capture the essence of it so well. Parent who are new to the nursery are frequently surprised and then fascinated if they arrive when a tray of gloop is out and being enjoyed by the children.

Equipment

Cornflour (approximately 6 tablespoons)
Water (approximately 100ml)
Food colouring
Large tray

Method

Pile about 6 tablespoons of cornflour in the middle of the tray and then gently add a little water, using your finger – or your child's fingers – to mix the lumpy flour into a paste. Keep it fairly stiff, so that there are patches of lumpy cornflour and some runnier puddles as well. Add a little more water until you have a fairly smooth mixture that you can manipulate and mix up, feeling the unusual texture as you play. Add food colouring as desired to give your gloop whichever shade you like.

Tips

This is a very enjoyable activity for all ages from 6 months upwards. With the babies we sit them in a high chair and put the gloop on to the tray in front of them. They can then put their fingers and hands in the mixture, enjoy feeling the sensation of it as it drops through their fingers.

Try to discourage them from eating it, but it is obviously quite safe if a little ends up being sampled. Gloop seems to appeal equally with older children and is actually quite good stress relief for adults, in a strangely addictive kind of way!

Angel Handprint Cards and Calendars

We have already touched on the delights of hand and footprinting and this is really a further extension of this, using the hand prints to make the wings of an angel to make a card or calendar. It is a great gift idea at Christmas and children can do it with differing degrees of independence depending on their age.

Equipment

A4 paper
A5 card (for cards) or A4 card (for calendars)
Ready mix paint or powder paint
Large paint brush
Scissors
Glue stick or PVA
Felt-tips or gold pen
Small calendar

Method

Using the paint, encourage your child to paint on the palm-side of one hand, covering it evenly. For smaller children, put the paint in a saucer and get them to dip their hand into it, but you may need to brush off any excess with a paint brush. Print the hand firmly down onto a sheet of white A4 paper and then repeat with the other hand. Once you are happy you have got a nice pair of handprints, clean up and leave the prints to dry.

In the meantime decide whether you are making a greetings card or a calendar. For the card, fold the sheet of A5 card in half to make a folded card. For the calendar, take a sheet of A4 card. Draw a triangular shape in the middle of the card, to resemble an angel's tunic. Then cut out the handprints carefully and stick them either side of the tunic, with finger tips pointing up and outwards, to look like angel's wings. Then use felt tips or your gold pen to add a head, halo, feet and any other finishing touches. Glitter is always popular and might add a sparkle to the tunic or halo. If you are making a calendar, fasten a small paper calendar to the bottom of the page.

Tips

Hand and foot prints can be used for all sorts of displays and activities. Try using brown and orange hand prints to make a tree shape in autumn and for Christmas time, use green handprints with red toes to look like holly or brown hand and foot prints to make reindeer. White footprints on black paper can be just as effective and great if you are talking about snow or to go with a story that involves following footprints, such as 'The Gruffalo'.

66

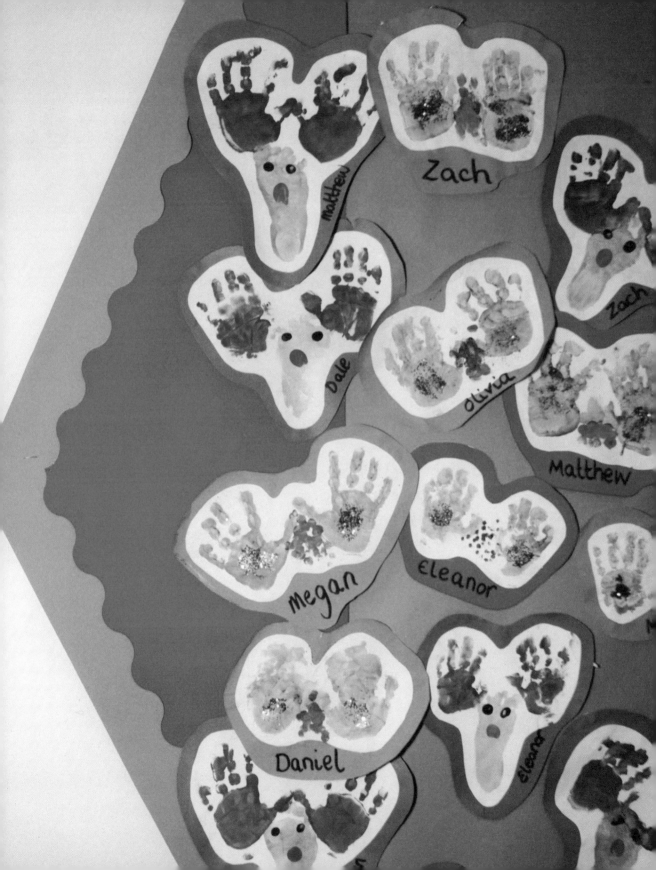

NATURE
AND
THE OUTDOORS

You can hardly pick up a paper these days without reading that children today get less time outside and have much less freedom than we had as children. However, the Early Years Foundation Stage gives us very clear guidance at nursery about how important it is that we plan an equal part of the curriculum to take place outside and see outdoor time as more than just an opportunity to run around or ride on bikes. So many of the activities in this book are suitable for doing outside, but this chapter concentrates on some particular outdoor projects and might give you a few ideas.

All children have different preferences for how and where they play and boys often need more physical activities and prefer being outside. My son has always been happy grubbing around outside and has spent hours amusing himself in the garden or out on walks, which is where many of these ideas came from.

Mini Beast Hunt

Most children are fascinated by creepy crawlies and enjoy watching bugs moving around. There are so many different possibilities for activities involving mini-beasts, including drawing and painting pictures of them, making models with pipe cleaners and even using plastic bugs in the sand tray or with bark chips. However, it is always good to have a purpose to a walk and this is a great way of getting children to walk a bit further or to be really observant when you are out.

Equipment

Clipboard and pencil
Magnifying glass
Bug viewer (if you have one)
Plastic container, such as a margarine pot, with a lid

Method

Before you set out on your hunt, discuss which insects you might see on your travels and make a list of those that you are hoping to find. You can make this more or less specific depending on the age of the children, but it is always useful to have a picture of the insect so you can make sure they know what they are looking for. A simple hunt might include a worm, a woodlouse and a spider, but you could add in a centipede, ladybird or daddy long-legs, depending on the time of year.

Go out for a walk, talking to your child about where each insect lives and introduce them to the idea of habitats. When you find one of the insects on your list, put it in the bug viewer if you have one, or temporarily in the pot, so that they can examine it with a magnifying glass and then draw it on their clipboard. When they have finished, set the insect free and move on to the next one on your list. When you have had enough, or when you have found all the insects on your list, return home and have a look at what you have drawn, talking about how the insect looked, felt and moved.

Tips

It is really important to provide your child with vocabulary which will support their language development and this in turn will help to reinforce understanding. Try to use interesting words when you are looking at the insects and their habitats and encourage your child to express their opinions and try out new words. When you get back you can develop this activity further with songs about insects (Incy Wincy Spider) or looking at insect books. Many companies now sell wormeries, antworks or butterfly gardens and these can be really enjoyable for children to watch and learn from.

Forest Pizzas

This activity does belong in this outdoors session, rather than the kitchen, despite the unlikely title! This was another Forest School idea and absolutely captured the imagination of all the children there.

Equipment

Paper plate
Ball of clay, about the size of your fist in
an airtight container (you can buy
modelling clay from many art and craft shops,
or use potter's clay if you have access to it, either is fine)

Method

Take your paper plate and wrapped ball of clay out with you for a walk, preferably to a woodland area, but anywhere with trees will do. Then, take the clay out and flatten it down to resemble a round pizza base and place it on the plate. Give it to your child and suggest that they are a pizza chef, looking for exciting toppings to put on their pizza. You might need to start them off with leaves, pine needles, saw dust, gravel etc but once they get going their imaginations usually run riot.

Tips

This activity leads on to so many more if your child is enthusiastic about the idea. When you return home this could be the focus for playing 'restaurants', using the pizza to talk about Italian restaurants and how pizzas are made. At nursery we might turn the home corner into an Italian restaurant, making our own menus and role playing what the waiters and chefs might say and do. You can still do this at home and might like to plan to make real pizzas for tea, so that you can talk about how you are using different shapes, textures and smells for the toppings, just as your child did with their forest pizza.

When you come to serve the pizza, it is, of course, a great opportunity to talk about fractions, gently introducing the concept of halves, quarters and eighths. Who'd have thought pizza was so educational – and fun?!

74

Bark Rubbing

Exploring textures and different surfaces is a great way of developing vocabulary and also to spark inquisitive thoughts like, "who lives under this rough stone?" Even in a built up area it is possible to find lots of different types of shrubs and trees and an afternoon of bark rubbing can be a great way to explore your local area.

Equipment

Plain paper (preferably white A4)
Wax crayons (the fatter the better)
Masking tape
Plastic folder
Glue stick
Piece of card or display paper

Method

Make a plan of where you are going to go with your child and talk to them about what sort of trees you might find and what sort of environment you might find them in. You could have a look in nature books or on the Internet and find out what the main types of trees look like. Older children might be able to suggest good places to visit or you might want to plan a trip to an arboretum or woodland area with them.

Once you find a tree, use masking tape to hold the paper onto a piece of fairly flat bark. Then use the side of the crayon to get a large surface and rub it gently over the paper, picking up the pattern of the bark as you go.

Find as many different trees as you can and take a rubbing from each. Store them in the plastic wallet and take them home, where you can then examine your results and cut them out to stick on a larger display. Depending on your child's stage of development, you might like to write out the names of the trees for them to cut out and stick on as well, or they may like to label the picture themselves, even if it is just with the first letter of the word.

Tips

Some local arboretums or National Trust areas have activity sheets that you can use to plan a trail through the trees and this can be a great basis for a bark-rubbing session. Follow a trail that you think will be a reasonable length for your child and don't forget to pack supplies to make it more of an adventure – hot chocolate and biscuits in the winter, or cold drinks and a snack in the summer. We are fans of Westonbirt Arboretum in Gloucestershire but see what you can find in your area.

Digital Camera Treasure Hunt

This is a more 21st-century version of the mini beast hunt, but it helps to introduce children to technology, or as it is now known within the Early Years curriculum, ICT (Information and Communication Technology). Even 2 year olds can be interested in the concept of taking photographs and looking at the results, but this is a real hit with children aged from 3 years up.

Equipment

Digital camera
PC to view the pictures on
Printer, if available
Paper and pencil

Method

You can theme this treasure hunt however you wish, so if you are in the middle of talking about autumn, you might wish to use that to help choose the items you are going to look for. Make a list on the paper of 10 items that you want your child to find, so for our autumn theme this might include: a dry leaf, a conker, a twig, a smooth stone, something orange, something brown etc. If you are able to include some indoor and some outdoor items this will add to the interest. Then show your child how to take a photograph with the camera and let them head off to hunt for the items on their list. You may well want to follow them closely with the list, so you can help them tick off the items as they record them, and also to keep an eye on the camera if it is not totally childproof!

Once you have completed the list, or have had enough, connect the camera to your computer and show your child the photographs. If you have a printer available, you can print them out and then use them to make a picture of what was found on your treasure hunt.

Tips

ICT is an important part of the learning environment for even young children and includes many types of toys and equipment, from electronic keyboards to walkie talkies and computer games. It is fascinating to see what children see through the camera lens and digital cameras have made it much easier for them to see the pictures that they have taken. They also quickly become familiar with what different pieces of equipment do and how they can manipulate them to get the best results. Remember when you are out and about to point out technology in action, for example, letting them press the button at a road crossing or getting the ticket out of a parking machine.

Colour Matching Cards

I spent a fascinating day at the Forest School Centre at Long Wittenham in Oxfordshire, which is where they train Forest School Leaders who take groups of children out in to the woods to learn through play. Several different activities were held whilst I was there, all of which were a huge hit with my children, who came along as guinea pigs. This is one of the easiest activities and can be carried out in a city park as well as in a large woodland area

Equipment

Coloured card, which is in natural shades,
e.g. greens, browns, oranges
Double-sided sticky tape
Scissors

Method

Cut out a large circle or oval shape on the card, or if you are feeling really artistic, a leaf shape. Don't go smaller than half a sheet of A4 or it can get a bit squashed later on. Cut 5cm strips of the sticky tape and fasten on to the piece of card in any pattern you like. Give your child a piece of prepared card, of different colours, and then challenge them to go out and fill each bit of sticky tape with something that is the same colour as the card. For example, if you had a dark green card, they could look for holly leaves, yew leaves, fir trees etc. If it is summer, you could use a yellow card and look for straw, hay, corn ears etc.

As the children find items, they peel off the top strip of sticky tape (keeping the strip to put in the rubbish) and fasten the item on to the card. You can keep this really simple with just 4 items for younger children, or go for 10 with older ones. Once they have filled one card up, they can always try a different colour as it will make them look again at the same surroundings.

Tips

This is another good way of developing observation skills. Children naturally show an interest in the features of objects and living things and you can encourage this interest by getting them to describe what they see and by helping them to find out more about the object. You can use questions and discussion in response to their signs of interest and this can lead to further investigation. This activity can turn a run around in the woods, or a walk in the park and make it into a really interesting and stimulating project.

Plaster of Paris Animal Prints

I have really fond memories of going on long walks as a child and stopping on the way round to make an animal print like these. My father would carry a rucksack with the ingredients in and it would make us all look really carefully at the tracks where we walked, to try and be the first to spot a suitable footprint. The plaster does take a while to dry, so you need to be prepared to walk for a bit longer whilst it sets, or maybe find a good picnic spot.

Equipment

A small plastic bowl
Plastic spoon
Plaster of Paris mix (available from craft shops or on the Internet)
Small flask of water
Cardboard strips and paper clips or a ring cut from a plastic bottle, such as
a large drink bottle, about 10cm deep

Method

Take your equipment with you for a walk in the woods or an area where you are likely to find wildlife prints, whether these are deer, badger, squirrels or birds such as crows or pigeons. Unpack your bowl and mix the plaster of Paris with the water, using the plastic spoon, according to the manufacturer's instructions on the packet. Place the plastic bottle section around the print, making sure that it is firmly pressed down into the ground, with no gaps. Or, if you are using cardboard strips, clip them together to make a collar and slide this into the ground instead. Pour in the plaster mix so that it is about 5cm deep and then leave it to set. This will take a minimum of 15 minutes, depending on the particular mixture.

When it is set firm, lift off the collar of plastic or cardboard and then lift up the set plaster. Turn it over and brush off any surplus mud. To highlight the print you can pick out the shape with brown or black paint.

Tips

This is a great way of exploring the outdoors and also carrying out a simple piece of science. The change in the plaster of Paris as it sets always interests the children and you can bring the print home and start a collection of different animal prints. If you are feeling less adventurous you can do this in the garden or even in the sandpit, using a pet or toy to make an imprint, then use the plaster in the same way. We have had some good dinosaur shapes which have been part of a larger project, so see what takes your child's fancy.

Growing Cress

This is a perennial children's favourite and couldn't be easier to do, but provides a real sense of satisfaction, as it works all year round.

Equipment

Cotton wool
Cress seeds
Water
Plastic tray from food packaging, or a yoghurt pot

Method

For the most simple version of this activity, dampen a layer of cotton wool and lay it in the plastic tray. Sprinkle over the cress seeds and then put it in a warm, light place, watering daily until the cress sprouts. This usually takes just a few days.

Tips

To extend learning with this activity, use it as a chance to talk about what plants need to grow and how you can examine that in a cress experiment. Make up 3 trays of cress seeds, one as discussed above, with water and light, then leave one without water but in the light and the last one put in a dark place, but water daily. At the end of a week, you can compare what has happened in each dish and it should reinforce the need for water and light.

Once the cress is a reasonable length, it is time to cut it and eat it. Generally children are more likely to try food that they have been involved in growing, so try a nibble of the cress on its own and then you could make egg and cress sandwiches for tea, encouraging the children to make up the sandwiches themselves, with a little help from you. Something as simple as buttering bread is a really good way of developing fine motor skills, so don't be tempted to do it for them, even if it is slow and messy!

Bird Cakes

These seed cakes for birds are simple to make and the children can really get involved in mixing them, enjoying the feel of the different ingredients in their hands. You can make them at any time of the year, but it is a really good winter activity and you could tie it in to taking part in the RSPB's annual bird watch, which involves counting and recording the birds you have seen in your garden on one particular day, usually in January or February. Don't forget to remind the children that this mixture is not edible and if you have any nut allergies, you can always omit the peanuts.

Ingredients

Mixed bird seed (from a garden centre or pet shop)
Sultanas, currants or raisins
Peanuts (from a garden centre or pet shop will be
cheaper than from a supermarket)
Grated cheese (any old bits from your fridge)
Lard or suet

Equipment

Yoghurt pot
String (at least 50cm length)
Large mixing bowl
Scissors
Wooden spoon

Tips

An activity like this can lead to a real Interest in birds and you can take it further to help your child to find out more. The internet is a great way of finding information so try having a look at relevant sites together; the RSPB (www.rspb.org.uk) has lots of information and activities for children and you could even get involved in events in your area.

At nursery we love getting involved in campaigns and fund-raising activities with lots of different groups, as it gives us a focus for a whole range of supporting activities and the children love feeling part of something that is happening in homes, nurseries and schools around the country.

Method

Start by making a small hole in your yoghurt pot with the scissors and then your child can thread the string through the hole, so you can knot it firmly on the inside. The knot does need to be large and secure, so that it doesn't slip through the hole once the weight of the seed cake is pulling it. Let the lard or suet come up to room temperature so it is soft enough to cut easily with a knife into small pieces. Put it in the mixing bowl and then add all the other ingredients. Now for the messy bit; squidge the ingredients together with your fingers until if forms a soft mass which you can push into the yoghurt pot. Don't rush this bit, the squidging is the best bit for the children and can be an enjoyable sensory experience!

Whilst you then have a good hot, soapy hand wash, the bird cakes can go in the fridge to harden up and set. This will usually take a couple of hours, but then they are ready to be hung up from a tree or bird table. Sometimes the 'cake' can slide out of the pots when you turn it upside down, in which case you tie a piece of string around the pot to hold it in when inverted. Now you can watch out for small birds such as tits and greenfinches and see if you can spot the odd woodpecker if you are lucky.

Welly Planting

There are so many planting activities that children enjoy, whether you have a window box or some tubs, or a large garden. Our nurseries vary hugely, with some in city centre locations, with limited opportunities for gardening, and some have their own large vegetable patches. However, whatever you have available, nothing beats the pleasure of watching something growing and then following its progress. Tomatoes, runner beans and courgettes are all favourites with the children, but they also enjoy planting flowers and watching them come into bloom.

Equipment

Old children's wellies
Stones or large gravel
Sharp knife
Compost
Bedding plants, either bought or grown
from seed - geraniums and begonias are ideal

Method

If you are growing the plants from seed, make sure they are at least 5cm high and ready to be planted out. This is an activity best carried out after the risk of frost has passed in late spring, when you might be putting summer bedding plants out in your garden. Explain to your child why you are doing it at this time and you can talk about frost and cold weather and what effect it has on plants.

Make a couple of holes in the sole of the welly with the sharp knife to allow for drainage. Also make a small hole at the top and back of the welly for hanging it up when you have finished. Then your child can fill the bottom of the welly with a shallow layer of stones, topping it up with some compost. Next put the plant into the welly, topping up with compost and pressing it down gently. You can now thread a piece of string through the hole at the back and suspend it from a tree, fence or even washing line, low enough that your child can water it. You will soon have a colourful display, which can be enjoyed by the whole family.

Tips

The novelty value of planting in old wellies adds to the sense of fun with this activity and when we did this the children loved identifying their own wellies and were much more motivated to go out and water them daily and follow their progress. It is a good way of studying how plants grow, explaining that they need water and sunshine and you might even like to make a simple weather chart, so that when you go out to check the plants each day you record whether it is sunny or wet, hot or cold.

Children love investigating the natural world and you can turn your outdoor area into a real learning zone by putting up wind chimes, streamers and windmills, to help explain about the weather. You could also take a pot of bubbles outside; these provide so much pleasure for babies through to adults and even small children can blow the bubbles themselves.

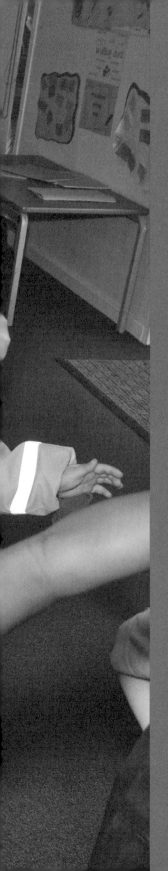

AFTER
SCHOOL
CLUB
ACTIVITIES

We have after school clubs at several of our nurseries, where children aged from 4 to 11 come to play and relax after a day at school. It is always a fine balance between providing fun and stimulating activities for them and allowing them time to unwind after a long day. If you have children of this age, you will know that they have a very clear idea of what they do or do not want to do, so we always plan topics and themes with them, based on what interests them and then ask them to choose what they would like to do every day.

School is a very civilizing influence on most children and really helps them to learn social skills and how to get on in a group. We find that group projects are really popular and the children will get together with a friend and get really stuck into something that they might not do on their own. My children tend to come home after school and if I don't distract them with something fun to do, the lure of the TV or the computer games can be irresistible. If your children have friends over to play, you might like to win some serious 'super parent' points by having a batch of pizza dough ready for them to put toppings on, or a pile of cardboard boxes ready for some junk modelling.

Body Outlines

Sometimes it is good to make something really big and you can't get better than making a life-size version of yourself. This activity allows children to make an elaborate self-portrait and then makes a great display for their bedroom.

Equipment

Large sheet of paper – preferably from a roll or the back of old wallpaper
Felt tips and crayons
Snippets of old material for collage
PVA glue
String or wool (hair coloured)

Method

Get your child to lie down on the sheet of paper and draw around his or her body outline with a marker pen. If you have more than one child, they can take turns at doing this to each other, as it always causes a lot of amusement and takes a lot longer than if an adult does it. Then you can decorate the outline as you wish, using paint, crayons, pens or collage. Children may enjoy choosing a favourite outline or sports kit and may like to use string or wool to represent their hair. When it is complete, cut around the outline and it will look really good on a bedroom door to announce who lives there.

Tips

We have done this within the After School Clubs to make whole teams up – either groups of friends from school, members of a football team or as part of a project on national costumes or holidays. You might not have room for quite so many at home, but making outlines of all the family – pets included at your peril – can be very entertaining and the children have a field day colouring you all in as they see you!

Moon Rocks

These are a real hit with our Holiday Club children, who can make them by themselves with limited adult supervision and they taste pretty good – remarkably similar to rock cakes really, but so much more interesting!

Ingredients

100g butter
300g plain flour
Half cup of raisins
100g sugar
1 egg, beaten

Equipment

Greased baking tray
Mixing bowl
Metal spoon

Method

Pre-heat the oven to 200C or 400F, gas mark 6. Using your fingers, rub the butter into the flour to make fine breadcrumbs. Add the sugar and raisins and then stir in the beaten egg. Using your hands, mix the ingredients to form a soft dough. Taking a small walnut-sized amount from the mixture, roll it into a ball and place it on the greased baking tray. Continue until all the mixture has been used, making sure the 'rocks' are well spaced out as they will spread during cooking. Bake for about 15 minutes, then allow to cool before placing on a cooling wire.

Tips

Cooking activities need to be carefully supervised for younger children, but as long as you are prepared to do a bit of clearing up, it is great to allow slightly older children a bit more freedom with their creations.

Try to encourage school-age children to weigh out the ingredients and to think about how the ingredients change when combined with other substances. Do let them taste and feel as they go and where possible talk to them about how the ingredients are made and where they come from.

You could always look at a world map and talk about where each ingredient is grown and how it ends up in our moon rocks. In my experience, cakes and biscuits are always most appealing fresh out of the oven, so try and arrange to make them just before tea, so you can insist on a sensible sandwich whilst they are cooling a little, but then you don't have to be too draconian about making them wait to try their results.

Junk Modelling

These days most of us are getting much better at recycling, but next time you have an interesting little box or container as packaging, put it in a separate bag or box and start to build up your own junk modelling supply. Loo rolls and kitchen paper rolls are fantastic, as are egg boxes, cardboard cartons and yoghurt pots. Bring these out on a rainy day and you have hours of fun guaranteed.

Equipment

Stapler
PVA glue
Ready made paint
Selection of cardboard tubes, boxes and plastic pots

Method

Use the various materials as building blocks to create a random object or to build a particular object. Glue or staple them together, depending on the weight and thickness of the item. Vehicles are always popular and jam jar lids make excellent wheels, as do lids from plastic pots. Egg box sections make good lights or bumpers and cardboard tubes are ideal for funnels. However, often children will just enjoy making random creations and they may decide what they look like when they finish.

Once dry, junk modelling can be painted and older children may wish to add finishing touches with dried pasta pieces or cut out pieces of tin foil or tissue paper.

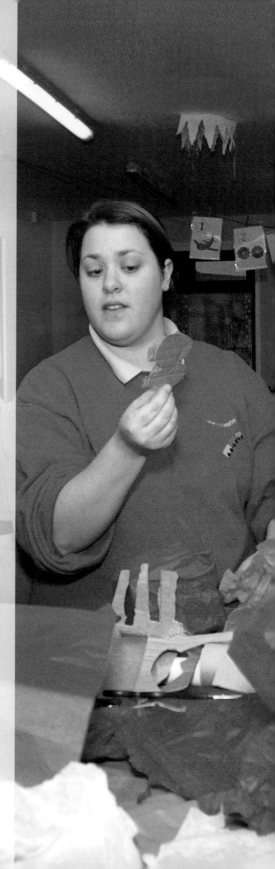

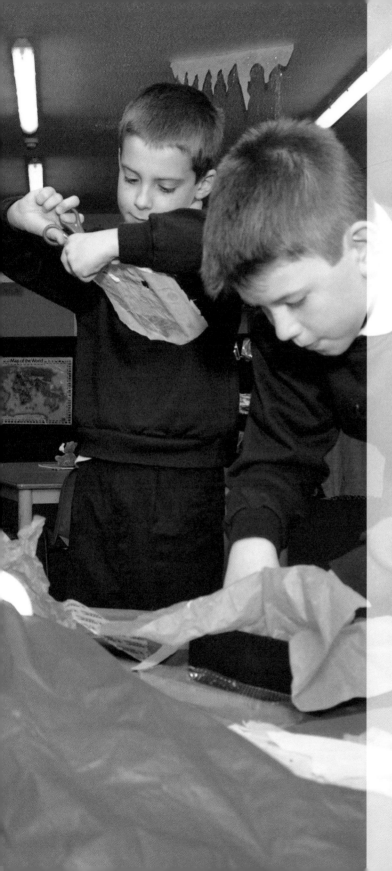

Tips

Junk modelling can be enjoyed by children as young as 2, with a little help, but still appeals to older children as they can use it to make specific models, such as cars or space ships. It is never the same activity as you can vary the items you have available, so keep an eye out for interesting things that you think would be useful.

It can fit in very well with other activities, so if you are talking about a particular topic, such as 'summer holidays', you could make something that was related, such as an aeroplane.

Junk modelling is also a really good group activity and you may find that older children enjoy working together to create a masterpiece. We have also had a lot of fun by giving the children a theme and then a set amount of time to produce something, which is judged by one of the Club staff. At home you might like to go for a 'Scrap Heap Challenge' event and give each child the same size and number of boxes and an hour to see what they can create. Remember to make a space to display their creations when they are complete, until they get too dusty and fall apart.

Den Making

Many of us may have very fond memories of making dens as children and it is a shame that these days many children have less opportunity for this sort of activity. However, with a little imagination dens can be created inside and outdoors and can provide hours of fun.

Equipment

A selection of:
Bamboo canes
Rugs, throws or blankets
Pillows and cushions
Tarpaulin or canvas
Chairs and benches
Bungees (elastic straps with hooks on the end)
Clothes pegs
Elastic bands

Method

This couldn't be easier as it simply involves giving a pile of equipment to your child or children and challenging them to make a den. Some will need a little encouragement and help them to think about how they can make a roof, walls, a door and even windows. If it is wet and you are inside, then the back of the sofa is a good start and you may just need to show them the basic principles of hooking something up to provide tension, or how to join 2 different items together with clothes pegs or elastic bands. However, do resist the urge to be too prescriptive and let them experiment – you can undoubtedly do it better than them, but they will feel a huge sense of achievement if they do most of it themselves.

Tips

Once the children have created a den, they often want to furnish it and use it for imaginative play. Whilst you may groan at the prospect of your best cushions being carted off down the garden to make seats, try and find some old alternatives and ask what they are to be used for – if you are asked for cushions for seats, would some spare bubble wrap do as well? Could you offer a picnic rug to act as carpet? For some reason, a den always needs food, so see whether a jug of water and a bowl of raisins might be welcome. If you possibly can leave the den up for a few hours, or even longer, it is really interesting to see how the children will use it next time. It may become something completely different and you may be required to provide a different set of props, but it is a lovely way to help develop imagination and to encourage creative thinking.

Sock Puppets

Puppets are popular with children of all ages and these are ones that you can make quite easily and then use for puppet shows or just as friendly new toys. I always seem to have an odd sock lurking somewhere which will do for this, or you can be really organised and keep a stash of them as the children grow out of old ones.

Equipment

Old sock
Buttons x 2
Wool
Needle and thread
Felt or scraps of fabric
PVA glue

Method

Start by deciding what your puppet is going to be; snakes are obviously very easy, but mice, cats and dogs are also fairly straightforward. The buttons need to be sewn on as the eyes at the toe end of the socks; older children may enjoy doing this themselves, but it is tricky due to the shape of the material and you may need to help out. Next add ears made from triangles of felt or material.

Depending on your sewing skills, you can either glue or sew on wool strands to make hair or fur and similarly make a mouth and nose using bits of felt or fabric. String or wool will also make a good tail, as will pipe cleaners if you have any. Once you have finished creating the puppet, he or she will need a name and then you are ready to play.

Tips

Puppets are a wonderful way to encourage imaginative play, as they allow children to create a new persona and make up stories without boundaries. You might like to make a very simple puppet theatre from a cardboard box with a cut out shape or your child might like to hide behind a chair or sofa to entertain you with a show from his or her puppet.

Pizza Making

Most children love to be involved in food preparation that results in them eating the final product. It is also a great way to get fussy eaters to be more adventurous and try different new ingredients. If you have plenty of time you can make the pizza dough yourself, either from scratch, using a packet mix, or in a bread maker. However, we normally do this after school (so that the children can eat it shortly afterwards), so we tend to use the ready made pizza bases that are available from the supermarket.

Ingredients

1 pizza base
2 tbsps tomato puree or passata
Selection of: sliced salami or chorizo, red or green peppers, olives, mushrooms, diced ham, sweetcorn, sliced tomato
50g grated mozzarella or cheddar

Equipment

Baking tray
Cheese grater
Sharp knife

Method

Turn the oven on to 200 C before you start and make sure hands are washed first - after a day at school this is particularly essential! The children can then spread the tomato puree on to the pizza base, leaving a gap of about 1cm around the edge.

They then need to add the toppings that they like, finishing off with the cheese. It is important not to overload the pizza or it will be soggy when cooked and the topping also needs to be evenly spread out so it cooks at an even speed.

When the creation is complete, lift it on to a baking tray and put it into the pre-heated oven for about 10 minutes, until the base is crisp around the edges and the cheese melted. Transfer onto a plate, serve and enjoy.

Tips

This is a great way of introducing the concept of 'Five a Day' to children of all ages and may be a good way of introducing different vegetables to your child. Sometimes vegetables that are not popular on their own can be more acceptable on a favourite like pizza when smothered with cheese. You could make a 'Five a Day' chart and complete it every day, discussing why fruit and vegetables are important for our health and how many different varieties there are.

Developing this theme further, you can also while away those long car journeys by playing Fruit or Vegetable alphabet, where each player has to take it in turns to name a fruit beginning with each letter of the alphabet: A for Apple, B for Banana, C for Cherry......etc, etc. It starts off easy, but does have some tricky parts. Back to the pizza – there is also lots of scope for budding mathematicians when it comes to dividing it into pieces, with discussion of angles and degrees.

Pub Cricket

Most of us will be familiar with some car games to pass the journey, such as 'I Spy', but this is one which is very popular in my family of cricket addicts. It might sound complicated, but bear with the explanation, as it is actually very simple and can really liven up a long drive. It is best played in towns and villages, so is not well-suited to motorway trips. Children from about 6 upwards will enjoy this and even if they find the scoring a challenge, you can encourage them to help with looking out for the signs, practising their reading and also with the adding up.

Method

This game is for 2 players, but you can always make teams up to include everyone. The first player is the batsman and the second is bowling. Each time you pass a pub, you need to look at the pub name and sign. Anything with a person or animal on it scores runs and anything with no people or animals is a fallen wicket. The body must, however, be complete. For example, The King's Arms is a wicket and not 2 runs because the' Arms' relates to a coat of arms and not the upper limbs!

Each limb on the sign counts as one run and in this game wings also count as limbs! So, a pub called 'The Angel' would score 6 runs, the 'Horse and Cart' would score 4 runs and 'The Fox and Hound' would score 8 runs. The batsman continues to accumulate runs as he passes these sort of pubs. Each time you pass a pub without any animals or people on the sign, the bowler takes a wicket. So, for example, after 'The Pegasus' and 'The Greyhound' the batsman is 10 for 0 wickets, but after then passing 'The Crown' and 'The King's Arms' he is 10 for 2.

This game does require a basic understanding of cricket scoring, but is pretty easy to pick up and can last for even the longest of journeys, as the bowler will need to pass 10 animal and human-free pubs before he bowls out the batsman. You can then swap positions and the bowler gets a chance to bat.

Tips

There are many games which involve using mental arithmetic, observation skills or memory. If this one doesn't appeal, try playing "'I went to the supermarket and bought..." where each player adds something to the list of shopping but must first repeat the whole shopping list perfectly. It can be played anywhere and is a great way of distracting bored children when you are in a queue for something and requires no equipment.

Another favourite in my family is 'name 10 things', for example, 'name 10 football teams in the Premiership', 'name 10 types of vegetable', 'name 10 animals with 4 legs'. The options are endless but can also be tailored for different age players.

Paint Bubble Planets

You will see earlier in this section a recipe for 'Moon Rocks' and these paper planets were made at the same time with our Holiday Club children, to follow a topic on outer space which included making their own rockets from cardboard tubes and tissue paper. We also looked at 'Google Earth' to see how our planet looked from space and it also lead on to making a display of some of the planets within the solar system. You can make this as involved as you like if your child has a particular interest in space, or you can just use the bubble painting to make some wrapping paper or a collage.

Equipment

Coloured paper
Powder or ready-mix paint
Fairy liquid
Plastic drinking straws
Tray

Method

Cut the coloured paper into different size circles, using plates as templates to help children with getting an even shape. Mix together the paint with washing up liquid, adding a little water if needed to get quite a runny consistency. Pour the paint mixture into your tray and then use a drinking straw to blow bubbles in it. Be careful not to suck by accident – you may need to have a chat about the difference between the two! Lie the coloured paper on top of the bubbles and then lift off. You should have lots of smaller circles decorating the paper. Experiment with different paper and paints and then you can layer the finished, dried circles to look like planets. You might like to use them to make a larger display or make a scrap-book of space, with each one labelled as a different planet.

Tips

Scissors can be a very emotive subject at nursery, as we all want our children to be able to use scissors effectively, but most of us are rather concerned about accidents occurring. We encourage pre-school children to have free access to scissors, with safety blades, so that they can help themselves to them whenever they need to cut something, in the same way that they have free access to pens, crayons, pencils and paper. However, with younger children you do have to be really vigilant and balance up the frustrations of the very 'safe' plastic scissors, which may not cut well at all, against watching carefully as they use more effective scissors.

Generally children adapt well to using whatever equipment is available to them, but I have once received a phone call from a distraught nursery manager, wondering how they were going to tell a parent that their daughter now had only one of the 2 hair bunches which she had started the day with.

Coat Hanger Mobiles

To continue on with our space theme, you might like to try making these mobiles. Obviously they can be designed around any theme you like and we have also made Easter mobiles and sports mobiles, depending on the interests of the children.

Equipment

2 wire coat hangers
String
Card – white or coloured
Colouring pens
Fablon or laminating pouches and laminator
Hole punch

Method

Using the paper draw a number of circles that will represent your planets, then use a book or website to establish what colour the different planets might be and which have rings around them. Clearly, older children may want to make a more detailed job of this, but even younger ones will enjoy colouring different circles and labelling them up as the planets.

Cut out all the planets once you have made enough, ideally about 8, but more is fine too. To make them last longer, cover them in fablon or laminate them, then use the hole punch to make a hole in the top of each one. Thread a length of string through each one. Take both coat hangers and slide one through the other to give a 4-armed shape, twisting the hooks together carefully. If the hangers are very brittle, it may be easier to cut the hook off one and use tape to fasten the 2 hangers together. The look you are aiming for is like the Advent Candle holder on Blue Peter – don't pretend you haven't ever seen it!

Fasten the string to the hangers, so that the planets dangle at suitable intervals and you can vary the length of string so that they can all be seen clearly. Your mobile is now ready to hang up and admire.

Tips

At our after school clubs we often find that the children are tired after a busy day at school and often want to do 'bite-sized' activities rather than getting stuck into a major project.

You might manage to complete a project like this in one go on a rainy day during the holidays, but don't be surprised if it might last over a week if you are doing a little after school every day. Try to set small targets, like researching the planets one evening, then starting on the colouring the next.

Labelling up the planets will help with spelling and general knowledge and may lead on to further discussion and research.

Be flexible and don't try to make it too formal, or they may feel like it's another school project. However, we seem to have many budding astronauts after doing this at one of our clubs, so it can capture the imagination.

CONTINUOUS PROVISION

One of the underlying principles of the Early Years Foundation Stage is that in order to help children to flourish, they must have the right enabling environment. This includes not just the physical environment they are in, but also the right atmosphere, loving adults and a good selection of appropriate resources.

There is no list of toys or equipment that you 'should' have for your children and many people would argue that our children these days are often overwhelmed by toys and games. However, we would expect to provide certain activities at all times at nursery, which children can choose to play with when they want to.

Obviously the degree of access to these activities depends on age and mobility and at home you simply can't have everything out all of the time, but if you are able to provide all of these activities at some time, your child will have some really great opportunities to learn through play.

Sand Play

Sand and water play are two of the activities which we have out all the time at nursery, as they are such a rich source of learning for children from toddlers upwards. At home you may not have room for a large sand pit, but you can still use a large tray and fill it with play sand. However, you do have to be prepared for it to go everywhere, so you may want to banish it to outside. It always amazes me how a small quantity can go a very long way! Older children may think they have grown out of sandpits, but you only have to see adults on the beach to know the attraction lasts for quite a long time, so it is also fun to get out for school age children.

Suggested resources

Large tray (a garden compost tray is ideal)
Bag of play sand (available from toy shops and garden
centres, it is cleaner and less abrasive than builder's sand)
Small rakes and trowels
Small flower pots
Fir cones
Pieces of bark
Small toys, cars, diggers etc

Activities

As with the water play ideas on page 118, keep a small selection of items in a 'sand box' to bring it out with the sand, such as the rakes and shovels or scoops. Then add in different items to see what develops; diggers and trucks can make an excellent building site, so you might want to introduce some Duplo or Lego. Dinosaurs or animals can develop into a farm or safari park, so you might need some bark to make fences and enclosures. Help your child to create different layouts and talk about how the sand feels, especially when you provide a jug of water to add it to the sand, which can then be moulded and piled up.

If you have more than one child, sand can be a good way to encourage co-operative play between them. See which resources capture their imagination and then prompt them to develop a theme between them. Praise both for their input and have extra bits and pieces to add if tensions arise or interest begins to wane.

Tips

You can really help to develop awareness of shape and space in these type of activities as your child will start to use positional language and understand whether something is 'bigger than' or 'smaller than'. Demonstrate some different words to extend the words that they already know and encourage them to talk about the shapes they see and use and where they are in relation to each other.

Water Play

Water is a magical medium for children and provides a fantastic opportunity to learn whilst playing. Most children love bath time, so you can build up a collection of resources to bring out at bath time, but then also take them out to use in the paddling pool or a bucket of water in the garden, or in a washing up bowl in the kitchen. This is really a set of suggestions for water play, rather than one particular activity, but might just get you to try something different.

Suggested resources

Yoghurt pots
Washing powder scoops
Empty washing up liquid bottles and small shampoo bottles
Plastic straws (especially 'curly wurly' ones)
Plastic funnels
Different sized plastic jugs
Food dyes

Activities

It is always good to have a basic set of toys that your child can use for water play; at nursery we would call this 'continuous provision'. However, to keep them interested and challenge their imagination, add a few extra bits and pieces each time you get them out, to see how they include these in their play and how they are used. For example, have a range of small bottles and lids, then add a small funnel and show how you can use it to fill the bottles. Next time, add a couple of different sized jugs, and use those to fill the bottles instead. This is an ideal time to introduce language about when something is empty, full, or holds more. Experiment with measuring quantities and seeing what the volume of each bottle is and when it will overflow.

Try colouring the water, either using special bath colours, or food dyes if you are using a bucket or large bowl. This can be really fun and of course, you can encourage the mixing of colours to see what the results are like. This might lead on to painting activities, or a combination of water play and painting, such as puddle painting.

Introducing ice cubes is another variation; tip a tray of ice cubes into the water and then watch them melt, seeing how a warm hand makes them melt quicker. Draw your child's attention to how the shape changes as the ice cube melts and talk about hot, cold, frozen and other language around temperature. Try to

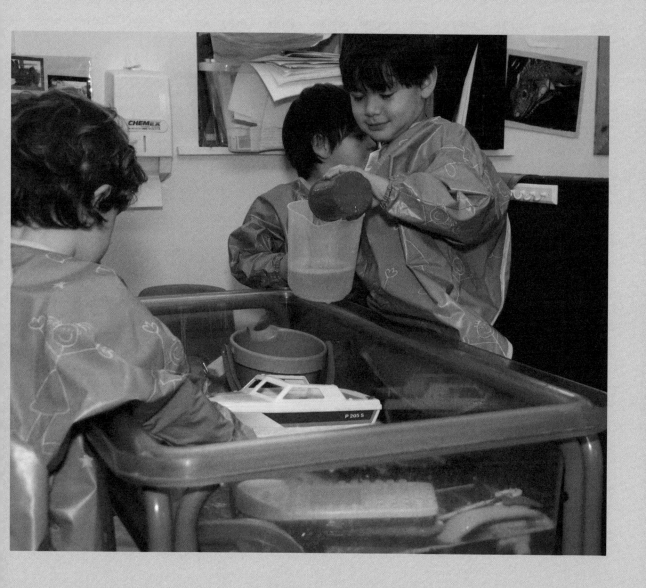

relate it to activities that you might have seen or done together, as this will help them to understand better, for example, you may have seen a programme about the Arctic, or been to the zoo and seen penguins. If you have any small plastic animals or insects, you might like to freeze them in yoghurt pots of coloured water; when you tip them out your will have your very own arctic scene to explore!

Rain is fascinating for children and whilst you can't beat going out to splash in puddles when it rains, you can also have a lot of fun recreating it with a hosepipe or watering can and an umbrella. On a smaller scale, make some holes in the bottom of a yoghurt pot and use it in the bath to talk about rain and the weather in general. By the time they are clean you will have covered the whole water cycle – detail depending on age and interest!

Information & Communication Technology

When children start school many parents are bamboozled by the term 'ICT' which is bandied around. In a work environment, most of us are familiar with the term 'IT' (Information Technology), but in an educational environment we add in communication, as it covers far more than just computers. Technology now plays such a major part in all our lives that it is really essential to introduce children to it from an early age. It can overlap with so many areas of play and learning within the nursery, both inside and out. It is easy to think of technology as being just the use of computers, but there are so many ways of introducing your child to the world of technology. Again, try and make these a part of every day activities, for example, when you are out for a walk, let them press the button on the pedestrian crossing and explain how it works. Listed below are a selection of games, toys and activities that help to introduce the concept of ICT, which they will take on into school with them.

Suggested resources

Walkie talkies – try having a game of hide and seek, using the walkie talkies to guide the seeker to the person who is hiding. Chat about people in the community who might use walkie talkies, such as the police.

Digital camera – you can buy children's cameras, but they can be fiddly and not have very large display screens, which the children can find frustrating. We tend to use simple mainstream digital cameras, although we do shop around for the most robust ones. The children quickly get the idea that they can see their image straight away on the small screen and love to have a look at what they have done. You can encourage them to photograph some particular activity, such as hunting for insects in the garden, or just ask them to take some pictures of their favourite toys or their best room in the house. You can upload the pictures onto the computer with them which provides a really great chance for discussion and for them to tell you what they are feeling and seeing.

Video cameras – can also be a lot of fun for children and particularly good for developing co-operative play with other children, although you may want to supervise fairly closely if your video camera is at all delicate. However, it can be surprising how children will recognise the need to be gentle with something precious and can really build their self-esteem if you let them use it, with clear ground rules in place.

Tape recorders / digital voice recorders / microphones – there are lots of products available that allow children to record sounds and voices. These can provide great entertainment and can encourage even the shyest child to take part.

Electric keyboards – again, these come in a range of prices and can be very simple or quite elaborate. There are also many electronic toy instruments, which can be fun, but may quickly drive you mad.

Torches are an absolute favourite and are great for exploring dark places inside and outside the house. You can also experiment with covering the end with different coloured tissue paper to change the light, or put them behind a piece of paper and experiment with shadows.

Old household items make great role play props, including mobile phones, calculators, keyboards, door bells and telephones. Children love imitating their parents and I have heard some truly fantastic conversations on the role play telephones!

Computers also have their place and there are many different pre-school programmes available, both as Internet downloads or on CD or DVD. We limit usage of the computer by using a large egg timer, or having a queuing system that the children understand; some children are not particularly interested but others will gravitate towards the screen, at the cost of other activities. You can get child-sized keyboards, which are great, but if you don't get anything else, do consider investing in a small mouse, as little hands really struggle to control a full-sized mouse.

Tips

Personally I have always loved it when my children opened Christmas and birthday presents that could be unwrapped and used straightaway without a hunt for batteries. However, there is a place for electronic toys and as long as you have a good selection of other non-electronic items, they really have their place in children's play and learning.

It may well be worth buying a battery charger sooner rather than later and stocking up on a range of re-chargeable batteries, so you don't always need to hunt around for replacements. Digital cameras that use batteries only and have no mains-charging facility can be really expensive and run out very quickly.

Construction

There is a lot of evidence from child development experts that construction play is a really important part of learning for young children. Most of us remember playing with wooden blocks, building with Lego or stacking up cubes or boxes. Now there is an enormous range of construction based toys available, but in practice it can be better to have one or two sets of really good quality construction materials, rather than lots of smaller sets of different types. At nursery we would try to have a large construction area and a small one, using equipment of different sizes. We would also have a construction area outside, to encourage different types of play in the outdoor environment.

Suggested resources

Large construction blocks, ideally wooden and hollow – a full set of blocks can cover a complex range of mathematical attributes.
Open ended recycled materials, such as cardboard tubes and cardboard boxes.
For outside play: crates, tyres, planks, ropes and string, washing lines and pegs, rugs and throws which can be used for enclosing a space.
Small construction sets of Lego, Duplo, Connex, Meccano etc. Try to find sets which will allow children to explore ideas such as enclosure, vertical/horizontal/diagonal lines and rotation.

Activities

Most children will not need a lot of adult interaction when it comes to construction play; however, you can encourage them by listening to what they are saying and making the odd suggestion, possibly about other resources they could add to their activity or by showing them a book or picture of something that they may be talking about. For example, you could find a picture of a castle, house, palace or vehicle and see if it helps them with their construction.

Tips

Construction play is really important as it gives children the opportunity to explore things, try something again and again and then reflect on what they have done and change it if they want to. It also helps with developing fine and gross motor skills; a pincer grip for moving smaller items, or larger muscle co-ordination to balance a plank between two tyres. They can play with another child, with you, or on their own and this can help them to learn to co-operate and share ideas to solve a problem.

If you don't have room to have lots of toys out all at once, try having a few different construction items in boxes and get them out at different times and in different combinations, supplementing them with some cardboard boxes or other household items like clothes pegs and lengths of rope.

Role Play

"*Let's pretend*" is one of the most powerful phrases when used with young children and role play is any sort of pretend play which allows children to recreate familiar experiences or enter completely new worlds. Children will either take on roles from their real lives, acting out family routines or familiar hobbies (this is known as 'sociodramatic' play) or they will create roles from their imagination (thematic fantasy play). If you are aware of both of these, you can provide the most appropriate props to encourage them with their adventures.

Suggested resources

Indoors:
Play kitchen area (can be cardboard boxes just as much as a plastic or wooden set).
Play food: either plastic, or preferably pieces of real fruit or play dough to use as part of a game.
Pots, pans and utensils (small 'real' items are much more enjoyable for children than plastic or specific children's items).
Dressing up clothes – there are lots of complete outfits available in the shops, but sometimes these can actually limit the imagination, so try and have pieces of material, capes, tea towels and scarves available that can be adapted.
Supporting books, magazines, price tags, notebooks and pens, old telephone or keyboards.

Outdoors:
Any of the above, plus equipment that is limited inside, such as buggies and pushchairs for dolls and teddies, shopping baskets, cars and bikes.
Also consider den-making equipment, such as blankets, broom handles, bamboo canes, clothes pegs, large cardboard boxes, string and ropes.

Tips

There is such a huge amount of play equipment available to buy that many parents feel that they have to fill their house and garden with equipment, that children lose interest in over time and can take up a huge amount of room. The good news is that the latest thinking in the Early Years arena is in favour of a return to natural materials and more 'real life' items, rather than masses of plastic.

Try to buy the most flexible resources that you can use for lots of different games – such as a small pop up tent or wigwam, or just save up the best large cardboard boxes. If in doubt, do read 'Crispin, The Pig Who Had It All' by Ted Dewan, a lovely modern fable of a small pig who had more material goods than he needed, but no friends to play with!

Method

When presented with a selection of role play equipment, some children will know straight away what they want to do and will just get on with it. You can make suggestions and add bits and pieces, but you may not need to do anything. However, if your child is not immediately interested, or you want to lead an activity, then you can set up a themed area together. Shops are always popular, so you can get out a selection of tins and packets, count out some money and make a shopping list together. This also brings in counting and writing skills, but all in a 'real life' context. Restaurants are also fun, as you can make a menu together, role play being the customer and the waiter and then write the bill.

Outside you can also encourage particular activities – den making, a doll's tea party, a car wash or a market. You might like to have some specific resources to reflect changes in the weather – a 'rain box' with umbrellas, watering cans, welly boots, or a 'barbeque box' with a small cooling wire to make believe as a BBQ grill, tongs and a brush and some pretend food items (toilet rolls, small cardboard boxes etc).

Rainy Day Box

Life with pre-school children can be exhausting and sometimes when you are at home with them on a wet day, with no plans, it can be a struggle to find something to do which everyone enjoys. This is where the rainy day box comes in, as you can have it tucked away for use in just such an emergency. Something new can capture a child's imagination and can also leave you feeling like a success!

Equipment

Large plastic or cardboard box
A selection of the following:
>New craft materials such as plasticine, unusual paint, gold or silver pens, stickers, felt shapes
>Coloured paper or card
>Animal masks
>Scarves or scraps of materials
>Art straws
>Packet of modelling clay
>Playing cards/UNO/matching pairs/memory game
>Selection of hats (have a look in your local charity shop)
>Tea towels or old sheets (to make capes)
>String

Method

You can break open the box when you need a little inspiration and either let your child choose a number of items, or perhaps ask them to close their eyes and draw a 'lucky dip'. You can then make some suggestions of activities that might follow on, such as particular craft activities, or you could give them a theme, such as 'pirates' or 'super heroes' and see what materialises.

Tips

Sometimes children need quite a lot of adult direction to get absorbed in an activity, whereas other times they will seize on an idea and you can just stand back and watch, providing more props as required. Many rainy day activities in my house seem to involve the need for food, so be prepared to find small bowls of raisins or other snacks which won't make too much of a mess. Teddy bears' picnics can be a great part of role play and might follow on from dressing up or den making.

Small World

Small world is the name we give to all types of miniature play, dolls houses, toy garages, zoos, farms etc. We try to have them out so that the children can select them whenever they want to, but at home you might find it easier to get them out at different times and maybe introduce new components to spark their imagination, such as some new animals or a new doll or two. Small world play offers children the chance to explore real and imaginary worlds in miniature and in their mind they too can live in a castle, be a bus driver, have an enormous family or whatever else they want to imagine. In their imaginary world they can be in control and choose what happens next........

Equipment and Method

There are many types of small world play, but this example just suggests how you can use this type of equipment to extend learning and get your child really involved in a particular topic or activity.

Set up a dolls house with a family of dolls – this does not need to be an elaborate house with expensive accessories, you can get some good strong cardboard ones, as well as all the plastic that is relatively inexpensive. Alternatively, you can make one with a large cardboard box and cut out windows and doors, this is often even more fun for the children and they can customise it better with paint, collage and drawings.

Ask them to tell you who each of the dolls is and think about adding new vocabulary, showing genuine interest in what they say and playing along with their imaginary family. You could then ask what the different members of the family do for a living and introduce concepts of the community to them; perhaps there is a policeman, a doctor, a hairdresser, a farmer or a teacher living there.

Then think about providing other props which can develop this theme further; perhaps some dressing up clothes or other toys which fit in as well. Encourage them to be inventive and you will help them to develop their imagination, by imitating what you do. You could then do some painting that flows on from the topic, or maybe go out for a walk to look at your local fire station, use a pelican crossing or watch a tractor in a field.

Any resources that support small world play should follow the interests of your child and try to consider the inhabitants of the small world, the landscape in which they are used and what containers you use to house the landscapes. For example you could use a large tray filled with sawdust or gravel to be a desert area and fill it with dinosaurs or wild animals. Keep the animals in a large box, that is labelled up with a picture of the animals, so your child can pull it out and choose what they want to use.

Tips

It is really important to get children to engage in imaginative and role play, based on experiences that are really familiar to them, so vary the activity depending on the interests and experiences of your own child. If you have more than one child, or have a visitor around to play, small world play is a really good way of developing co-operation, as the children gradually learn to take turns and share and will enjoy developing a story together. This can develop into all types of role play fun and can also help to nurture a less confident child.

They will also be able to develop their narrative skills, both with indoor and outdoor role play; they could be a waiter in a restaurant taking orders and mark making (pretend writing), or they could be a farmer in a tractor in the garden sowing seeds and checking on animals. Help them by suggesting good descriptive words and offering extensions to the storyline.

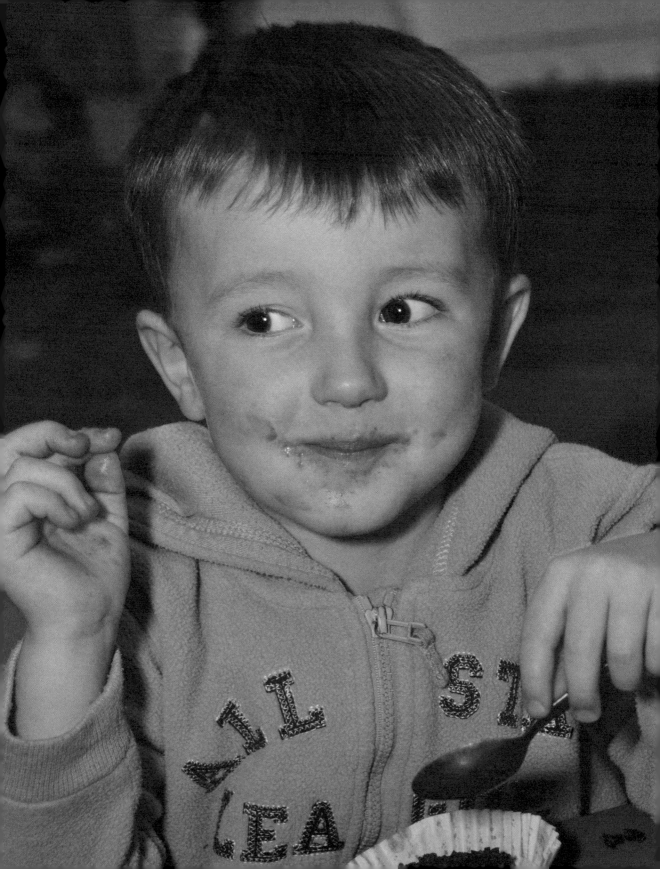

COOKING
AND
FOOD
ACTIVITIES

Now I must confess at this point that my life before nurseries had largely revolved around catering, so the food that we serve at the nurseries has always been a subject close to my heart. It seems such a shame to keep food preparation as an activity separate from children, as it is such a vital part of life and a great skill to have as well.

We start baking with the children from toddler age up and if nothing else, they like licking their fingers and scraping the bowl....don't we all?

I know that many of these recipes are sweet rather than savoury, but they are all very popular and easy to make. If you can get an early love of baking and shaking, you can quickly expand your child's repertoire whilst learning about mathematical concepts and basic science, then you get to eat it. Happy baking!

Piggy Biscuits

You may not always feel like a major baking session, or you may be entertaining more than one child and need an activity which is less stressful with several small messy people! If you have a few ingredients in your kitchen cupboard, you can easily do this activity without any forward planning. At nursery we often have a 'biscuit decorating activity' out at open afternoons and parties, with one member of staff overseeing it. The results are usually sticky, colourful, but a lot of fun!

Ingredients

Pack of digestive biscuits
Ready-roll icing (white)
Red food colouring
Raisins
Icing pen or a little jam

Equipment

Rolling pin
Bowls for mixing colour into icing
Different size circular cutters

Method

Separate your icing into 3 parts; one will be white; one light pink and one dark pink. Colour your icing accordingly with the red food colouring, but do use sparingly or your pigs will look rather sunburnt! Roll out and cut the icing; a large dark pink circle (face), one medium sized light pink circle (nose) and 2 small white circles (eyes). Place the dark pink circle on to the biscuit using the jam or icing pen to stick it down. Then add the nose and eyes, sticking down in the same way. To finish, dab the raisins with jam and place on the pig's nose for definition. Oink! Oink!

Tips

You could try baking your own biscuits first, to extend this activity for older children. Read the 'Three Little Pigs' before you start and then talk about it together as you make these biscuits. Go and visit some pigs on a local farm or animal park and try using some new descriptive words, perhaps concentrating on comparative size, shades of colour or noises. For example; small, smaller, smallest or on top, under, beneath. If you can't face a messy session, try this activity with different coloured paper and glue.

Chocolate Cornflake Cakes

These are another classic cooking activity which I didn't feel we could leave out. It is incredibly easy and the children really can do all of it themselves. You can vary the recipe by adding nuts or raisins if you want to, but the basic version is always popular and can be eaten pleasingly soon after making.

Ingredients

200g plain chocolate
3 tbsps golden syrup
50g butter
100g cornflakes

Equipment

1 x muffin tin with paper cases
Large heavy based saucepan
Large mixing bowl
Wooden spoon

Method

Break the chocolate into squares and then place in the saucepan with the golden syrup and butter and melt gently. Take off the heat and stir in the cornflakes with a wooden spoon. Children love watching the cornflakes getting coated in the sticky chocolate and can then spoon the mixture into the paper cases, before the all-important licking of the bowl. Leave to cool completely then enjoy!

Tips

You can make a very easy variation of this recipe by melting 100g of toffees with 100g of butter and 100g marshmallows. Then add 100g of rice crispies and mix well. You can either make this in individual cases as for the cornflake cakes, or grease a 23cm square brownie tin and press the mixture into this instead. Again, cool well then cut into squares. These are great cakes to make for birthday parties, which your children can actually be involved in making.

Peppermint Creams

Every Christmas for the last 5 years I have been persuaded to go and make peppermint creams with the infant class at my children's school. Whilst it is very simple, it seems to have a real appeal to even the youngest children, with the added benefit that the mixture is yummy. These make great presents and can be wrapped up decoratively to look quite professional. Owing to the delicate colour of the mixture and the fact that it isn't cooked, I am always very fussy about the level of hand washing that takes place before we start!

Ingredients

500g icing sugar, sieved
2 egg whites, beaten until frothy
Half a tsp of peppermint essence

Equipment

Large mixing bowl
Wooden spoon
Rolling pin
Trays lined with baking parchment
Cutters

Method

Sieve the icing sugar into the bowl and then add the egg white and peppermint essence to a well in the centre and gradually draw in all the icing sugar, until you have a firm dough. This does take quite a bit of mixing and is good if you have several children helping as they can all have a turn. It is important that the final dough is not too sticky as it will be really difficult to roll out.

Dust the table lightly with icing sugar or cornflour and turn the mixture out. Roll it out to a thickness of about 5mm and cut out whatever shapes you like. Small shapes are best, without too many sticky-out bits, as the finished creams will be quite brittle and likely to break. I have found that stars and circles work well. Lift the creams on to the parchment paper with a palette knife and leave to dry for 24 hours.

Tips

You can then package the peppermint creams up in cellophane or small boxes and they will keep well for a couple of weeks. If you want a more grown-up version, you can dip the mints into melted dark chocolate and then leave to harden on the parchment paper. They make delicious after-dinner mints.

Gingerbread Men (and Women!)

This is just a simple gingerbread biscuit mixture, so if you have a collection of cutters that you use for playdough or cooking, you can use them for making these biscuits. However, it is worth investing in a gingerbread boy and girl cutter, as children seem to enjoy these most and you can have fun decorating them afterwards if you wish.

Ingredients

100g butter
175g brown sugar (soft light brown or Demerara is best)
4 tbsps golden syrup
1 egg, beaten
1 tsp bicarbonate of soda
2 tsps ground ginger
350g plain flour

Equipment

Large mixing bowl
Large metal spoon
Rolling pin
Baking sheets, lightly greased
Cutters

Tips

You may like to give the gingerbread men eyes and buttons made from currants, in which case these need to be pushed gently into the mixture before they go in the oven. If you want to use the biscuits as hanging decorations for the Christmas tree, make a small hole in the biscuits before they go in the oven. Once they are cool you can make a simple icing mix, from icing sugar and water, then pipe it onto the biscuits to make faces or other decorations.

Method

Pre-heat your oven to 190 C or gas mark 5. Sieve the flour, bicarbonate of soda and ginger into the bowl, then add the butter, cut into small cubes. Rub the butter into the flour mixture until it resembles fine breadcrumbs. Try and encourage your child to do this themselves, explaining that they should try and keep their palms clean (to avoid it getting very squidgy) and think of making a rain shower of flour as they gently rub their fingers together. It will take a bit of practice but they will eventually get the hang of it. You may need to finish off, just to make sure there aren't any big lumps of butter, as these will make the biscuits a bit greasy.

Stir the sugar into the mixture, then add the beaten egg and syrup and mix well with the metal spoon. Draw the mixture together into a dough and place it onto a floured surface and knead it gently. The dough is fairly forgiving and can cope with quite a lot of handling before the finished biscuits suffer too much! Try to remember that it is the activity that is most important and that your little chefs won't be too picky if the resulting biscuits are not as short as they could be.

Once the dough is smooth, roll it out to about 5mm thick. You may find it easier to cut it into 2 halves and to roll each one out separately, flouring underneath as you go. Then cut out whatever shapes you like and place them on the baking tray, with a small space between them. Bake in the oven for 12-15 minutes, depending on how thin they are, then cool for 5 minutes on the sheet before lifting on to a cooling wire.

Pomanders

These traditional scented gifts go back a long way, but still seem to provide entertainment and a great sense of achievement. They smell lovely hung in the kitchen and can be made by even small children. They are also reputed to be good moth repellents if hung in a wardrobe, but I would suggest that you dry them out well in the kitchen before you try this. Make sure you use really fresh oranges, or the skin gets really tough and little fingers find it hard to get the cloves in.

Equipment

1 x orange
Packet of dried cloves
Length of ribbon, about 50cm long and no more than 1cm wide
Masking tape

Method

Cut the masking tape to the same thickness as your ribbon and use it to make a criss-cross shape on the orange, running from top to bottom like lines of longitude around a globe. This is where the ribbon will go later. Then take the cloves and push them into the orange to cover all the peel that is showing. They should be just touching each other, so that you can't see any orange in between cloves. If your child is finding it difficult, you might need to use a skewer or knitting needle to make small holes, but usually they can manage to push them in themselves.

Once the orange is completely covered in cloves, remove the masking tape and loop the ribbon tightly around in its place. Tie it at the top and make a loop for hanging. Your pomander is now ready and can be hung up in the kitchen or a warm place to give off a lovely scent.

Tips

Using cloves is a great way of introducing spices and herbs to children. You could get out all the spices you have and smell them, talking about how you use them. It is also interesting to look at how they grow and where they come from and could be a prompt for getting an atlas out to look at the countries of origin.

Very Easy Vanilla Fudge

This is a great recipe for 2 year olds upwards and can come in very handy as a gift around Christmas, birthdays or any other celebrations that children like to be involved in. You might consider investing in a roll of clear cellophane from a craft or gift shop and by the time you have wrapped up your offerings in a square of cellophane and decorated it with a ribbon, even the most amateur baking can look really good!

Ingredients

175g softened butter
175g condensed milk
800g sieved icing sugar
(and extra for rolling out)

Equipment

Rolling pin
Mixing bowl
Wooden spoon
Table knives
Medium sweet (petit four) cases

Method

Place softened butter and condensed milk in a bowl and gradually sieve in the icing sugar. Mix it together to form a dough-like texture and knead until it is smooth and easy to handle. Roll out the fudge with a rolling pin, using icing sugar to prevent it from sticking on the table. It should be about 1cm thick and you can then cut it into squares of shapes as you like. Place the fudge shapes into the cases and leave overnight to set.

Tips

For a slightly stronger taste, add a few drops of vanilla essence to the mixture, or use food colouring if you would like a different colour. You can also add dried fruit – I love dried cranberries and blueberries and these can be more popular with children than raisins or sultanas. You can also dip the fudge into melted chocolate, or for a real children's favourite, decorate with a chocolate button. If you have some biscuit cutters these can also be used to follow a particular theme – holly leaves for Christmas, pumpkins for Halloween – let your imagination run riot!

Flapjacks

Flapjacks are incredibly easy to make and children can get really involved, with very little adult intervention. I have tried many different recipes but find that this one gives a good consistency that doesn't set too hard.

Ingredients

450g rolled oats (you can add cherries, nuts, seeds, chocolate chips, coconut, whatever you fancy, just make the total weight 450g)
75g brown sugar
300g unsalted butter
3 tbsp of golden syrup

Equipment

1 x 23cm square baking tin, lightly greased with oil or butter
Small heavy based saucepan
Large mixing bowl
Wooden spoon

Method

Preheat your oven to 190 C or gas mark 5. Melt the butter with the golden syrup gently in the saucepan. In a large bowl mix the oats with the sugar, then add the melted mixture and stir well. Press the mixture into the prepared tin and cook for approximately 20 minutes, when it should be golden brown. Leave to cool for a few minutes before marking into pieces, but leave it until it is completely cold to cut up and take it out of the tin.

Tips

Porridge oats can be really interesting for children, who usually enjoy tasting them raw and can also use them for messy play activities – they make a great desert for burying dinosaurs or plastic insects in. They also become fascinatingly sticky when mixed with water and can then become 'mud' for the dinosaurs. It is easy to forget that food items can make great play mediums, but you might also try crushed weetabix, baked beans or spaghetti hoops. Aprons and a handwash bowl are essential, but you might be surprised how much fun you can have with them!

Chinese New Year Food Tasting

One of the areas that is covered in the Early Years Foundation Stage is 'Knowledge and understanding of the world'. Children are like sponges and soak up new information, so it is a great time to introduce them to other cultures and it is no surprise that they are always interested in the food of other cultures. We have held all sorts of different food tasting sessions, but one of the most popular is part of a celebration of Chinese New Year. *Kung Hei Fat Choi!*

Ingredients

A selction of:
Prawn crackers
Egg fried rice
Sweet and sour pork
Tinned bamboo shoots
Fresh beansprouts
Spring rolls
Fortune cookies

Method

Invite a friend round for tea and lay up your table for a Chinese New Year feast. You might like to make pretend menus beforehand, copying Chinese letters from a book or the Internet, either painting them or drawing them. Try and find some chopsticks, just to give your child an idea of how they are used. If you have any fancy dress clothes, these add to the occasion, but then just lay out all the food and encourage the children to taste each dish, telling you how it tastes and feels. Try everything yourself, as the children are much more likely to try different tastes if they see you doing the same.

See if you can find any pictures of the dragon dances that are used to celebrate the New Year and after your feast you might like to make a dragon mask and find a sheet to drape over the children; we have had a lot of fun at nursery with pretending to be dragons and dancing to Chinese music.

Tips

Even babies can be involved in food tasting, as they love to put things in their mouths and explore with all their senses. Try putting a wipeable mat on the floor, put your child on it in a nappy and vest and surround them with a whole orange, lemon and lime. Then put down a chopped up orange, lime and lemon and let them explore how they all feel and taste. They are often surprisingly keen on the tangy limes and lemons, and can really be interested in the smell, taste and feel of the fruits.

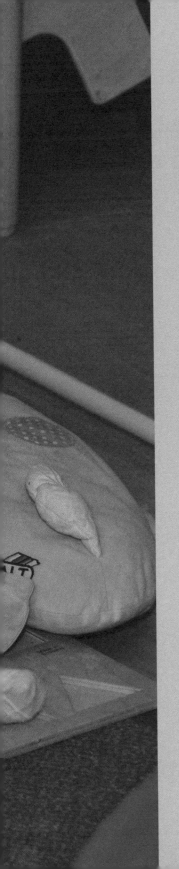

IDEAS
FOR THE
UNDER 2s

Many of the suggestions in this book will apply to children aged from a few months upwards to at least 5 year olds, but as babies have such differing needs, it seemed only right to include a chapter focussing on the needs of Under 2s. As a parent you will be aware of how fast they grow and develop at this stage, becoming aware of themselves as separate beings, discovering what they like and dislike and exploring their surroundings constantly.

There is such a huge amount of equipment and toys available, but as a parent I was fascinated by some of the activities that my 6 month old son did at nursery, as I would simply never have thought of it. The citrus fruit tasting is a case in point, as included in this chapter.

Similarly, whilst I thought I knew lots of nursery rhymes and songs, I found I was sadly out of date and needed a little bit of refresher training, so we have included a few current favourites in this chapter too. Most of all, I hope you will have fun with your baby with some of these activities.

Herb Bags

The sense of smell is a powerful one and develops from a very early age. So many toys for children concentrate on sound and feel and smell can be missed out easily, other than particularly at mealtimes. This activity is so easy to do but can be good fun and has many different variations to maintain your baby's interest.

Equipment

Large mixing bowl
A selection of small fabric or net bags – the ones that come free with
 washing powder are ideal
A selection of fresh and dried herbs and/or spices
(only larger dried ones, such as cinnamon sticks, nutmegs and bay leaves)

Method

Simply divide the herbs up and fill the bags with single varieties of herbs and spices, tying them off securely and making sure there are no loose strings that could be dangerous. You can then either place the bags in a basket and encourage your baby to take one out and show them how to smell it, scrunching it to release the smell more, or you can put a row of pegs up and hang the bags from them, at a height where your baby can reach them and feel them to release the aroma. A simple mug tree can also be used to hang the bags off and makes a really good alternative to a treasure basket as your baby can explore it at their own pace. You will need to make sure that they don't actually eat the bags, but usually they will find the flavours too strong and the texture unappealing, but will enjoy exploring the smell and texture.

Tips

You can have fun with smell with toddlers as well; try filling old socks with cotton wool and scent it with different things. Essential oils such as lavender or geranium are great, lemon oil or rosewater (both available in the supermarket), also ground coffee, perfume, after-shave, soap or grated candles. Tie the socks up tightly and have a guessing game, to see if they can identify the smells.

Pre-schoolers also enjoy making fragrant flowers; place a ball of cotton wool in a petit four case (or make larger ones in normal paper cake cases) and stick it down with some glue. Then scent the cotton wool with different fragrances – old perfume, lavender oil, fruit essences etc and paint them if desired. Then fasten the 'flower' onto a plastic straw and place it in a plastic vase or cup to make a bouquet of flowers. When we've made these at nursery the children have returned time and again to try and work out what they all smell of and compare the different scents.

Citrus Fruit Tasting

Even babies can be involved in food tasting, as they love to put things in their mouths and explore with all their senses. We have had some really fun session with this activity; as long as babies are able to sit up unsupported they can join in and I have even seen after-school club children joining in as they think it looks so entertaining. Try putting a wipeable mat on the floor, put your child on it in a nappy and vest and surround them with a whole orange, lemon and lime. Then put down a chopped up orange, lime and lemon and let them explore how they all feel and taste. They are often surprisingly keen on the tangy limes and lemons, but can really be interested in the smell, taste and feel of the fruits.

Equipment

Plastic mat or wipeable surface
A selection of whole oranges,
lemons, grapefruit and limes
Knife and board
Bowl of warm water and
flannel for afterwards

Method

Unless you fancy extra washing, strip your baby down to his or her nappy and make sure the room is warm. Put your baby onto the mat and then give them a few of the whole fruits to feel, touch and put in their mouths. Then cut one of each of the fruits into quarters and put them down as well. Sit and watch as they explore each piece, discovering the different smells, textures and most importantly, taste.

Talk to your baby while playing and suggest words for how they might find the fruit, 'sharp, tangy, sweet, juicy' and so on. Older toddlers may try some of the words out themselves and this really helps to build their vocabulary and language skills. For smaller babies, enjoy their facial expressions and take your lead from them. Once they have had enough, give them a good wash and return to the clearing up when you have a chance.

Tips

Babies respond differently to different sounds that they hear and from an early age they can distinguish patterns of sound. There has been much debate recently about the disadvantages of buggies that face away from the parent, as this does not encourage parents to talk to their children. An activity like this gives a great opportunity to communicate and help your baby to learn to talk by being talked to by you.

Rhymes

Rhymes are a lovely way to engage with your baby whether they are excited and playful, quiet and thoughtful or sleepy and in need of a cuddle. There is something for every occasion and they can be a really special time between you both. It can also be something to share with anyone else who may care for your baby at different times, as it can be a familiar and soothing part of their routine. For small babies, chant rhymes whilst rocking them in a chair or crib, or say one when changing their nappy to keep their attention and entertain them. For older babies and toddlers, vary the rhyme to their level of activity and be as energetic as they are!

Some favourite rhymes for babies:

Round and round the garden
Round and round the garden, like a teddy bear
One step, two step (move your fingers up to their neck)
Tickly under there (tickle under their chin)

This one is great for nappy change time if your baby doesn't like lying down, as you can distract them with the rhyme and turn a grumble into a giggle.

An elephant goes like this and that
An elephant goes like this and that
She's terribly big
And terribly fat
She has no fingers
She has no toes
But goodness gracious
what a nose!

This rhyme continues with the ever-popular animal theme and even small babies will enjoy listening to your voice as you say this rhyme, using actions to add to the drama. Stretch your arms out to show how big the elephant is and how fat. Touch your toes and your baby's toes and fingers as you describe those and then finish up by tickling them on the nose. As with *Round and round the garden*, they will quickly anticipate your next move and will soon be able to identify their nose, toes and fingers when you ask them where they are.

Horsey, horsey

Horsey, horsey, don't you stop
Just let your feet go clippety clop
Let your tail go 'swish' and the wheels go round
Giddy up, we're homeward bound

Singing and rhyme is a great time for close physical contact with your baby as many of the rhymes can be done with your baby on your lap. Many of you may remember *This is the way the lady rides* from your own childhood; this is another equine rhyme with lots of actions that babies love. Bounce them gently up and down during rhyme, maintaining eye contact throughout so they feel secure, then lift them a little higher on the 'giddy up' at the end. The sound of the words can also be enhanced with a bit of percussion if you are feeling enthusiastic – coconut shells make great 'clip clops' and a rattle or rainmaker can be good for the 'swish' of the wheels.

Teddy bear, teddy bear

Teddy bear, teddy bear, touch your nose
Teddy bear, teddy bear, touch your toes
Teddy bear, teddy bear, turn around
Teddy bear, teddy bear, touch the ground

Many children have favourite bears and they can be used in this rhyme to show your baby what to do. Toddlers are often fascinated with their own bodies and quickly learn to point out their own features, so will join in with this one. You can add extra verses depending on the time of day, so for example at sleep time you could say,

Teddy bear, teddy bear, time for bed
Teddy bear, teddy bear, lay down your head
Teddy bear, teddy bear, turn off the light
Teddy bear, teddy bear, say goodnight!

Tips

Many parents feel a bit self-conscious when they first go along to music groups or baby groups and have to sing or say rhymes in public. Often we are a bit rusty and can't remember half the words, but the children's enjoyment is usually enough to overcome initial embarrassment and it is amazing how quickly the words come flooding back. There are some great tapes and CDs available, not to mention whole on-line libraries of favourite songs and rhymes that you can download for free, so the sky is your limit!

Fabric and Scarves

Many babies have a comfort blanket or muslin or some other piece of much-loved fabric which is their special comforter. You can build on this enjoyment of the feel of fabrics by having a collection of scarves or pieces of fabric which you bring out for a special play time together.

Equipment

Basket or container
Selection of scarves – ideally silk, wool, cotton, crêpe, in fact, anything you can find at your nearest charity shop, jumble sale or car-boot sale.
Odd pieces of fabric you may have at home, or samples from a fabric shop or upholstery shop – different textures such as tweed, velvet and corduroy are ideal.

Method

Get the basket out when your baby is alert and playful and start with a game of 'peekaboo', covering your face with a piece of material, then pulling it down and saying "Boo". After a couple of goes your baby will soon get the idea and you should get lots of smiles. Then try draping the scarf over your baby and get them to pull it down, saying "Boo" as you do, helping them if they need it.

Once they are enjoying this, try giving them different pieces of fabric to feel and talk to them about the different textures and whether it feels smooth or rough. Let them pull out pieces from the basket and see which is most popular. If they are mobile, try putting on some salsa music or something up-beat and encourage them to dance around with the scarves, seeing how they fly in the air as you toss them up. If you have more than one child involved, particularly if your baby has an older sibling or friend, they will love watching the movement of the scarves and watching what the older child does with them.

Tips

Something as simple as this can really help babies to develop their fine motor skills as they use a pincer grip to hold the fabrics and choose which one they want. If they are already starting to pick up pieces of food with their fingers then this is a good way of developing their co-ordination further, but they also love the movement, colour and feel of all the materials. Do use the scarves for other play times too; try getting them out for some singing or rhymes and incorporate them into a favourite nursery rhyme – how about using a sparkly scarf to wave during Twinkle, twinkle, little star *or something more nautical for* The big ship sails on the alley-alley-o *?*

Song Time

Many children start to use words between their first and second birthdays and singing with your child can really help them to experiment with words and sounds in a fun way. Don't be at all concerned if they get so engrossed in the actions or making sounds with shakers or their hands, that they forget to sing as well. It takes a while for them to co-ordinate all of this at once (as it may with you!), but repetition will help them to acquire the skills.

Equipment

You obviously don't need more than your voice for a simple singing session, but a little like the Story Sacks we feature in the 'Sounds, words and numbers' chapter, it may be handy to have a small basket of props that you can use when singing if you have them to hand. Suggestions include:

A wand with a star on it – Twinkle, twinkle, little star
A rag doll – Miss Polly had a dolly
A toy sheep – Baa, baa black sheep
A toy spider – Incy, wincy spider

Your child will soon start to link the toy that you get out with the song that you are going to sing and it all helps them to develop the connections which are so useful as they grow.

A selection of percussion instruments is also great to have, start with home-made shakers and add small cymbals, bells and drums. You can buy these relatively inexpensively from shops and you can often pick them up at sales as well.

Suggested songs:

Head, shoulders, knees and toes

Head, shoulders, knees and toes, knees and toes, knees and toes
Head, shoulders, knees and toes, knees and toes,
And eyes and ears and mouth and nose,
Head, shoulders, knees and toes, knees and toes.

Touch each of the parts of the body as you sing this song and then for each subsequent verse miss out one part of the body, replacing it with a '*mmm*' noise. As you child gets older they will join in more and more and with older children it is fun seeing who remembers which word they are supposed to be missing out.

Miss Polly had a dolly

*Miss Polly had a dolly who was
sick, sick, sick.(cradle a dolly)
So she phoned for the doctor
to be quick, quick, quick.
The doctor came with his
bag and hat,
And knocked at the door
with a rat a tat tat.
(make a knocking motion)*

*He looked at the dolly and
shook his head,
(shake your head)
And said "Miss Polly
put her straight to bed."
(waggle your finger)
He wrote on a pad
for a pill, pill, pill.
(make a writing motion)
I'll be back in the morning
with my bill, bill, bill.*

Dingly, dangly scarecrow

*I'm a dingly, dangly scarecrow
(put your arms out and act
like a rag doll)
With a flippy, floppy hat.
(adjust your imaginary hat)
I can shake my hands like this
(shake your hands...)
I can shake my feet like that.
(shake your feet...)*

More Song Time

She'll be coming round the mountain
She'll be coming round the mountain when she comes
She'll be coming round the mountain when she comes
She'll be coming round the mountain, coming round the mountain,
She'll be coming round the mountain when she comes.

She'll be driving six white horses when she comes
She'll be driving six white horses when she comes
She'll be driving six white horses, driving six white horses
She'll be driving six white horses when she comes.

Oh, we'll all go out to meet her when she comes
Oh, we'll all go out to meet her when she comes
Oh, we'll all go out to meet her, all go out to meet her,
Yes we'll all go out to meet her when she comes.

She'll be wearing red pajamas when she comes
She'll be wearing red pajamas when she comes
She'll be wearing red pajamas, wearing red pajamas,
She'll be wearing red pajamas when she comes.

She will have to sleep with Grandma when she comes
She will have to sleep with Grandma when she comes
She will have to sleep with Grandma, have to sleep with Grandma,
She will have to sleep with Grandma when she comes.

This song my seem lengthy, but you can change the verses as you
wish and can vary the tempo as you go, speeding up and slowing
down. It is a great song to bounce your child on your knee to and
they will enjoy the repetition and speed, like a galloping horse.
Encourage older children to add their own verses and personalise
it, using their own names and family members as they like.

Treasure Baskets

Treasure baskets are a collection of everyday objects with different textures, shapes, sizes and smells that babies can explore safely. Throughout time babies have been given real objects to play with, such as keys and wooden spoons and through playing with these they have learnt about the world around them. Children have always enjoyed collecting 'treasure' to play with, from special shaped stones and pebbles, shells and coins; today's children may have many toys, but all sorts of interesting items can be valued and enjoyed.

An educationalist called Elinor Golschmidt carried out research with children under 3 and found that offering a range of natural and household objects, that they could explore on their own with adult interaction, helped them to develop. It is easy to gather a selection of objects into a basket at home and then review it on a regular basis to keep it fresh and exciting. It is obviously really important to make sure that all the objects are safe for the age of your child and cannot be harmful in anyway, especially when they end up being chewed.

Equipment

Items in a treasure basket should help your child to work out what different items will do: stretch or not stretch, make a sound when shaken or remain silent, stay rigid or bend. Unexpected responses are great and can cause real delight, particularly when you share the discovery with them and smile back. Try a selection of items from the list below:

A piece of emery paper
A bunch of keys
A loofah
A wooden honey dipper
A large pine cone (make sure none of the pieces are loose)
Wooden curtain rings
A non scratch cleaning pad
Wooden spoons
A wooden nail brush
A wooden and cotton washing up brush
A wooden pastry brush
A wooden spaghetti measurer (with different sized holes)
Wooden bangles or bracelets
Small shaker or percussion instrument
Leather juggling balls

Method

Put all the objects in a basket and place it down in front of your baby. Sit with them and encourage them to explore the objects, showing them what different things do and letting them touch and feel each object. However, try not to interfere too much if they are happily exploring and let them set the pace, which may include only examining one item for some time and completely ignoring others.

Tips

Schema are patterns of behaviour that can be observed when young children play; these are particularly evident with babies and toddlers who are enjoying a treasure basket, as you will see them enveloping or wrapping one item in another, or carrying one object to a different place and then on to another. These repetitive activities play a crucial part in brain development and are therefore great to encourage.

CD Mobiles

In our baby rooms we always try and have a lot of displays at baby level, so that they can really see and enjoy different colours and fabrics and can watch items move in the breeze. Many babies will have mobiles over their cots when they are tiny, but for safety these are usually moved once they are able to pull themselves up and get tangled in them or break them. However, babies love to watch dangling objects and those that glitter or catch the light are very attractive. These are a great way of using up old CDs which you may have around the house or office.

Equipment

Old CDs, about 10
Clear fishing line or cotton thread
Scissors

Method

Thread the fishing line or cotton through the centre of the discs and join 5 of the CDs together in a long line, depending on the height of your ceiling. Do this twice, to give you 2 'chains' of CDs and then fasten them from a light fitting, hook or door frame to dangle above your baby when they are sitting in a favourite area or on a rug, but do make sure that they can not reach them and pull them down or get tangled in them.

If you want the mobile to be more portable, fasten the string onto a metal coat hanger and then you can hang it anywhere in the house that your baby might be.

Tips

If you hang the mobiles near to an open door or window, they will provide even greater entertainment as they move and clink in the breeze. You may like to let toddlers decorate the CDs with glue and glitter, before you thread them up, for extra interest. If the children enjoy the noise of the 'clinking', then try giving them metal spoons or small percussion instruments to try to replicate the noise. You can also use the CDs to decorate a tree in the garden – they are fairly weather proof and easy to take down when you want a change.

Sound Line

You can buy lots of elaborate mats and toys for babies that have sounds incorporated in them, but it is also easy to introduce everyday sounds at home, in a way that is easy to update as they grow and develop.

Method

Attach a wooden curtain pole or an old towel rail to the wall at an accessible height for your baby. Use short lengths of string or cord to attach a variety of objects to the rail so that they can be banged, rattled or shaken to make a range of different noises. The sort of things you might like to try include:

> Small metal saucepans
> Metal colander or sieve
> Bells
> Lengths of beads
> Milk bottle tops threaded onto a piece of string
> Conkers
> A metal whisk or spoons
> Plastic drinks bottles with rice or dried pulses inside

You can also attach a line outside to a fence or between 2 shrubs and hang the objects from that. You may feel like you have a scrap yard rather than a back garden, but it provides a great exploring zone and can stimulate all sorts of experimenting with the different sounds each material makes, especially when hit with different implements, from sticks to wooden spoons or metal spoons. You can change the items regularly and depending on what your child really likes and to keep them re-visiting to see what is new. If your child is just at the 'cruising' stage of learning to walk, then this can help them to pull themselves up and balance while they explore the different objects.

Tips

Babies take great pleasure in making and listening to a wide range of noises and soon begin to create their own sounds which will then become words. Try to listen to what they say and 'tune in' to their messages; if they make a noise with one of the objects on the sound line that they are really pleased with, then help them to make it again and show that you are sharing their pleasure by smiling and talking to them about the sound. This helps them to feel valued and enriches their enjoyment of the games.
It is sometimes easy to forget that babies understand a great deal more than they can express, so ask them to repeat an action or make a noise that you noticed they liked and they will often be able to do so and will be really pleased with themselves.

HISTORY

THE OLD STATION NURSERY LTD

The Old Station Nursery Ltd is a childcare company I set up when I couldn't find the right sort of care for my own children. They were 2 and 4 at the time and I had just left a career in the Army to move to Oxfordshire. I started to research nurseries and attended some business start up courses and then in May 2002 purchased an old railway building in Faringdon, Oxfordshire. We opened the doors to children 2 months later. We were providing day care for up to 60 children aged from 3 months to 8 years, serving home cooked meals with organic vegetables and offering pre-school French classes and music sessions, in a homely, caring environment.

Since then the company has gone from strength to strength. In 2004 we bid for a contract to run the nursery at RAF Benson in Oxfordshire and were delighted to win. The success of this contract led to interest from other RAF stations, including RAF Waddington and RAF Cottesmore and at the same time I saw a group of 3 nurseries in Lincoln city centre advertised in the trade press. I thought these would tie in well with the RAF sites we were hoping to operate.

I made an offer for the 3 nurseries, which was accepted in spring 2006 and then soon after won the contracts to run the Waddington and Cottesmore nurseries. By October 2006 we had 5 nurseries in Lincoln and Rutland. Then we took over the nursery at Newark College and subsequently Gainsborough College, followed by RAF Linton-on-Ouse, near York and Filkins Nursery in Oxfordshire. Most recently, we took over the operation of another site in Lincoln, known as our Lincoln Waterside branch, which is in the same building as a gym company.

The Old Station Nursery Ltd employs over 250 people and offers a range of career opportunities, from NVQ training through to degrees in Early Years and Childcare. Our nurseries offer a 'home from home' for children in a range of different settings; just within Lincoln we have huge variety as Wragby Road is a converted house, Lincoln College is in the old courtrooms, The Marina is an airy new-build and Waddington is a large old building within the camp perimeter. Each has a slightly different feel but with the same high standards of childcare, so parents can choose the enviroment that best suits them and their children.

During our years of operation we have been widely recognised with both industry and general business awards, for providing excellent day care in a challenging economic environment. We have also been awarded the Investors In People standard, reflecting the importance we place on all our staff and their personal development. In 2008 we won the Nursery World's Business Development Award and were short-listed in their national awards as one of the top three nursery chains. It is a real pleasure to be at the helm of such a great company.

There is a great deal of childcare available now and parents must look around carefully to find what suits them and their child. However, all parents are interested in what their children do during the time that they are at nursery and this book aims to give a few suggestions and ideas which might be fun to carry out together at home. I hope you will all enjoy a lot of mess, creativity and laughter as a result of reading this book; I remember being told to make the most of the early years, when your child actually says, "Will you play with me?" as before you know it they will be teenagers who are far too cool for that!
Enjoy them while you can......

THANKS

The list of thanks for producing a book like this could run to many pages, but first and foremost I must thank Mazz for her patience and good humour in photographing all the children who have featured in the book. Life at nursery is frequently fairly lively and she coped admirably with the changes to plan that are associated with working with children. She quickly understood what I was hoping to achieve and has taken some lovely photographs which really capture the essence of the fun that can be had with children.

Thanks, of course, to the children themselves who were such fantastic models. The names of all the children, our special little models, are on the next page. Although some were a little shy at first, many of them couldn't get enough of the camera and insisted on frequent checks of the digital images, just to see how they looked.

All the managers and staff of the nurseries involved were fantastic at rustling up the ingredients, organising the activities and cajoling less willing participants to join in. They all coped with the general chaos that we caused and I thank them all for their support with this project. I couldn't ask for a more dedicated team of staff and I hope this book will be a real celebration of what they do on a daily basis.

Finally, thanks go to my long suffering family, especially my husband Kirk, who put up with me disappearing off to write another chapter when I could be spending more time with them instead.

For many years I have been juggling the demands of running The Old Station Nursery with trying to be a good mother and wife; at times the balance may have been slightly off, but I hope the results are worth it in the long run. I couldn't do any of it without a great support team of family and friends; I hope you all enjoy the book too.

Thanks to all our special models

Benson Nursery
Aaron
Archie
Caitlin
Caitlin
Carol
Casey
Chloe
Craig
Denise
Ella-Louise
Elliot
Gabriela
George
Iain
Ieuan
Isla
Jamie Lee
Joshua
Kathryn
Lace
Lewis
Matthew
Mia-Grace
Oliver
Owen
Owen
Rebecca
Seren
Shantel
Sofia
Sophie
Stacey
Thomas

**Buckland
After School Club**
Ben
Claudia
Connor
Elysia
Emily
Hannah
Harry
Jessica
Saskia

Faringdon Nursery
Ciaran
Heidi
Isis
Jessica
Jodie
Joshua
Kacey
Kayleigh
Karima
Maddy
Mathilda
Melanie
Olivia
Rachel
Siena
Thomas

Filkins Nursery
Aaron
Alexander
Benedict
Beth
Charlie
Elizabeth
Fletcher
Hugo
Joshua
Lucy
Oliver
Thomas
Toby

Lincoln College Nursery
Aeryn
Charlotte
Ellie-Ann
Grace
Imogen
Jack
Lewis
Mia
Naomi
Nikhil
Oliver
Tyler

Marina Nursery
Edward
Fletcher
Lola
Mariam
Michael
Nathan
Noah
Oliver
Olivia
Poppy
Zane

Newark College Nursery
Emma
Haidon
James
Rocco
Saint
Samson
Tommy

Wragby Road Nursery
Erin
Grace
Lewis
Ruby
Aymen
Megan
David
Harvey
Jack
Tia
Savannah
Ruby
Cameron
Dominic
Elizabeth
Owen
Nicholas

INDEX

SARAH STEEL

Sarah founded The Old Station Nursery Ltd in 2002, after a search for high quality local childcare left her thinking that there was a gap in the market. She says that her 'Eureka' moment was after looking round numerous nurseries that she didn't really like but had huge waiting lists and thought 'I could do better than that'. There have been challenging times since then, but it has undoubtedly been a success story.

Sarah was awarded Lincolnshire 'Outstanding Woman in Business' in 2007. Other awards include 'Inspirational Business Mum of the Year' and finalist of 'Oxfordshire Business Person of the Year' in 2007, and finalist in 'Growing Business Female Entrepreneur of the Year' in 2008. The company won 'Winning Business' in the Lincolnshire Business Awards in 2007, 'Business Development' in the 2007 Nursery Management Today Awards and 'Business Development' in the 2008 Nursery World Awards.

Sarah is a member of the Department for Schools, Children and Families Children's Plan Expert Group and also a member of their Early Years Stakeholder Group, both of which advise Government on policy around Early Years and Education. She is actively involved in the childcare sector and is a member of the National Policy Executive for the National Day Nurseries Association. She is also a keen advocate for Women in Enterprise and is part of the BERR Women Ambassador's programme and has also attended BERR workshops to advise on Government support for women in business.

Sarah is a director of the not-for-profit company Communities in Business, which provides support for people from non-traditional business backgrounds during their first 2 years of setting up a business. (the website www.communitiesinbusiness.org.uk can provide further information). She has also been involved in mentoring other women in pre-start up and start-up business through the SEEDA Enterprise Gateway scheme.

However, Sarah would say that her greatest achievement to date, other than staying sane, is bringing up her two children, Harry and Jessica, who are now 10 and 8. They were her inspiration for starting the company in the first place and have both attended nursery and after-school and holiday clubs within the company, providing first-hand customer feedback. They have tried and tested most of the activities and recipes in this book and would definitely guarantee the fun that is lurking within!

USEFUL WEBSITES

www.childcarelink.gov.uk
A good site to search for childcare of all types within the UK, by region or postcode.

www.greenshop.co.uk
The Greenshop, based in Gloucestershire, is one of the UK's leading environmental retailers.

www.henry.org.uk
A website designed for early years practitioners and other health professionals who work with families, to advise them on infant and child nutrition. Lots of really interesting research to read.

www.imperfectlynatural.com
Janey Lee Grace shares her pick of the best natural and holistic ideas for a more natural, chemical free and eco-friendly way of living, plus the website has as a thriving parenting forum.

www.ndna.org.uk
National Day Nurseries Association seeks to develop, encourage and maintain high standards in education and care for the benefit of children, their families and their local communities.

www.ofsted.gov.uk
Read reports on all childminders and childcare settings.

www.payingforchildcare.org.uk
Use this site to see how you can benefit from help available with childcare fees, whether you are working, studying or at home.

www.rspb.org.uk
Excellent download for information about animal prints, to go with our 'plaster of Paris animal tracks' page. Other great activities for children related to birds and wildlife.

www.standards.dfes.gov.uk/eyfs
Read more about the Early Years Foundation Stage and understand what it means to your child.

www.stop-the-rot.co.uk
A website dedicated to encouraging good dental hygiene for young children. We follow this scheme at all our nurseries.

www.theoldstationnursery.co.uk
Information on all our nurseries and links to other useful organisations for parents.

www.workingfamilies.org.uk
Great information site for working parents about allowances, benefits and advice on balancing work and family responsibilities.